Everyday
Mediterranean

pil

Publications International, Ltd.

Photographs on front cover, pages 93 and 145 and art throughout copyright © Shutterstock.com.

Pictured on the front cover: Mediterranean Chicken Kabobs *(page 144)*.

Pictured on the back cover *(top to bottom)*: Greek Salad *(page 46)*, Beans and Greens Crostini *(page 26)* and Minestrone Soup *(page 44)*.

ISBN: 978-1-63938-545-4

Manufactured in China.

8 7 6 5 4 3 2 1

Let's get social!
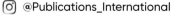 @Publications_International
@PublicationsInternational
www.pilbooks.com

Table of Contents

Egg Dishes

Basil-Feta Frittata

MAKES 4 SERVINGS

8 eggs

¼ cup plain Greek yogurt

¼ cup chopped fresh basil

¼ teaspoon salt

¼ teaspoon black pepper

1 tablespoon olive oil or butter

1 cup crumbled feta cheese with basil, olives and sun-dried tomatoes or plain feta cheese

¼ cup pine nuts (optional)

1. Preheat broiler. Beat eggs, yogurt, basil, salt and pepper in medium bowl until well blended.

2. Heat oil in large ovenproof skillet over medium heat, tilting skillet to coat bottom and side. Pour egg mixture into skillet; cover and cook 8 to 10 minutes or until eggs are set around edge (center will be wet).

3. Sprinkle feta and pine nuts, if desired, evenly over top. Transfer to broiler; broil 4 to 5 inches from heat source 2 minutes or until center is set and pine nuts are golden brown. Cut into wedges to serve.

Shakshuka

MAKES 6 SERVINGS

¼ cup olive oil

1 medium onion, chopped

1 red bell pepper, chopped

3 cloves garlic, sliced

1 can (28 ounces) crushed tomatoes with basil, garlic and oregano

2 teaspoons sugar

2 teaspoons ground cumin

2 teaspoons paprika

½ teaspoon salt

¼ teaspoon red pepper flakes

¾ cup (3 ounces) crumbled feta cheese

6 eggs

Chopped fresh cilantro or parsley (optional)

1. Heat oil in large skillet over medium-high heat. Add onion and bell pepper; cook and stir 5 minutes or until vegetables are softened. Add garlic; cook and stir 1 minute. Stir in tomatoes, sugar, cumin, paprika, salt and red pepper flakes; mix well. Reduce heat to medium-low; simmer 25 minutes, stirring frequently. Stir in cheese.

2. Make six divots in tomato sauce; crack one egg into each divot. Cover and cook 15 to 18 minutes or until egg whites are set but yolks are still creamy.

3. Scoop eggs and sauce into serving dishes; sprinkle with cilantro.

Mediterranean Frittata

MAKES 4 MAIN-DISH OR 8 APPETIZER SERVINGS

¼ cup olive oil

1 large or 2 medium onions, thinly sliced

1 cup chopped fresh tomatoes

6 eggs

4 ounces prosciutto or ham, chopped

¼ cup grated Parmesan cheese

2 tablespoons chopped fresh parsley

½ teaspoon dried marjoram

¼ teaspoon salt

¼ teaspoon dried basil

⅛ teaspoon black pepper

2 tablespoons butter

1. Heat oil in large skillet over medium-high heat. Add onion; cook and stir 8 to 10 minutes until soft and golden. Reduce heat to medium. Add tomatoes; cook and stir 5 minutes. Transfer vegetables to large bowl; cool to room temperature.

2. Beat eggs in medium bowl. Add to onion mixture with prosciutto, Parmesan, parsley, marjoram, salt, basil and pepper; mix well.

3. Preheat broiler. Heat butter in medium broilerproof nonstick skillet over medium-low heat until melted and bubbly. Add egg mixture; cook 8 to 10 minutes until all but top ¼ inch of frittata is set. (Shake skillet gently to test.) *Do not stir.*

4. Broil frittata about 4 inches from heat source 1 to 2 minutes or until top is set. (Do not brown or frittata will be dry.) Cut into wedges. Serve warm or at room temperature.

Spinach, Pepper and Olive Omelet

MAKES 2 TO 4 SERVINGS

2 tablespoons olive oil, divided

1 cup diced red bell pepper

½ teaspoon dried rosemary

⅛ teaspoon red pepper flakes

2 cups loosely packed baby spinach, coarsely chopped

16 stuffed green olives, such as manzanilla, sliced

2 tablespoons chopped fresh basil

8 eggs

3 tablespoons milk

½ teaspoon salt

2 ounces crumbled goat cheese or feta cheese, divided

1. Heat 1 tablespoon oil in medium nonstick skillet over medium-high heat. Add bell pepper, rosemary and red pepper flakes; cook and stir 4 minutes or until soft. Remove from heat; stir in spinach, olives and basil. Transfer to medium bowl; cover and let stand 5 minutes for spinach to wilt slightly.

2. Meanwhile, beat eggs, milk and salt in another medium bowl until well blended. Heat remaining 1 tablespoon oil in same skillet over medium heat. Pour half of egg mixture into skillet. Cook 3 to 5 minutes or until eggs are set around edge, lifting edge to allow uncooked portion to flow underneath.

3. When egg mixture is set, spoon half of spinach mixture over half of omelet. Top with half of cheese. Loosen omelet with spatula and fold in half. Slide omelet onto plate; cut in half. Repeat with remaining ingredients.

Shortcut Spanish Tortilla

MAKES 4 TO 6 SERVINGS

- 2 tablespoons olive oil
- 1 medium onion, cut in half and thinly sliced
- 10 eggs
- ½ teaspoon salt
- ⅛ teaspoon black pepper
- 5 ounces potato chips (use plain thin chips, not kettle), lightly crushed
- Chopped fresh chives or parsley (optional)

1. Preheat oven to 350°F. Spray 8-inch round baking pan with nonstick cooking spray. Heat oil in medium skillet over medium-high heat. Add onion; cook and stir 5 minutes or until onion is softened and beginning to brown. Remove from heat; cool 5 minutes.

2. Meanwhile, beat eggs, salt and pepper in medium bowl until blended. Add potato chips; fold in gently until all chips are coated. Let stand 5 minutes to soften. Stir in onion until well blended. Pour egg mixture into prepared pan; smooth top.

3. Bake 25 minutes or until toothpick inserted into center comes out clean. Remove to wire rack; cool 5 minutes. Loosen tortilla from side of pan, if necessary. Invert tortilla onto plate; invert again onto large serving plate or cutting board. Garnish with chives.

Kale Quiche

MAKES 4 TO 6 SERVINGS

1 tablespoon olive oil

1 small onion, chopped

1 clove garlic, minced

1½ cups packed thinly sliced stemmed kale

¾ teaspoon salt, divided

8 eggs

1 cup (4 ounces) shredded mozzarella or Swiss cheese

¾ cup whipping cream or plain Greek yogurt

¼ teaspoon black pepper

1. Preheat oven to 350°F. Spray 8-inch square baking pan with nonstick cooking spray.

2. Heat oil in medium skillet over medium-high heat. Add onion; cook and stir 5 minutes or until softened. Add garlic; cook and stir 1 minute. Add kale and ¼ teaspoon salt; cook 10 minutes, stirring occasionally. Set aside to cool slightly.

3. Beat eggs, cheese, cream, remaining ½ teaspoon salt and pepper in medium bowl until well blended. Add kale mixture; mix well. Pour into prepared pan.

4. Bake 30 to 35 minutes or until toothpick inserted into center comes out clean. Cool in pan on wire rack; let stand 10 minutes before serving.

Frittata Rustica

MAKES 2 TO 4 SERVINGS

4 ounces cremini mushrooms, stems trimmed, cut into thirds

1 tablespoon olive oil, divided

½ teaspoon plus ⅛ teaspoon salt, divided

½ cup chopped onion

1 cup packed chopped stemmed lacinato kale

½ cup halved grape tomatoes

4 eggs

½ teaspoon Italian seasoning

Black pepper

⅓ cup shredded mozzarella cheese

1 tablespoon shredded Parmesan cheese

Chopped fresh parsley (optional)

1. Preheat oven to 400°F. Spread mushrooms on small baking sheet; drizzle with 1 teaspoon oil and sprinkle with ⅛ teaspoon salt. Roast 15 to 20 minutes or until well browned and tender.

2. Heat remaining 2 teaspoons oil in small (6- to 8-inch) ovenproof nonstick skillet over medium heat. Add onion; cook and stir 5 minutes or until softened. Add kale and ¼ teaspoon salt; cook and stir 10 minutes or until kale is tender. Add tomatoes; cook and stir 3 minutes or until tomatoes are soft. Stir in mushrooms.

3. Preheat broiler. Whisk eggs, remaining ¼ teaspoon salt, Italian seasoning and pepper in small bowl until well blended.

4. Pour egg mixture over vegetables in skillet; stir gently to mix. Cook 3 minutes or until eggs are set around edge, lifting edge to allow uncooked portion to flow underneath. Sprinkle with mozzarella and Parmesan.

5. Broil 3 minutes or until eggs are set and cheese is browned. Cut into four wedges. Garnish with parsley.

Small Plates

Tirokafteri
(Spicy Greek Feta Spread)

MAKES 2 CUPS

- 2 small hot red peppers
- ½ small clove garlic
- 1 block (8 ounces) feta cheese
- ¾ cup plain Greek yogurt
- 1 tablespoon lemon juice
- ½ teaspoon salt
- Toasted French bread slices and/or cut-up fresh vegetables

1. Preheat oven to 400°F. Place peppers on small piece of foil on baking sheet. Bake 15 minutes or until peppers are soft and charred. Cool completely. Scrape off skin with paring knife. Cut off top and remove seeds. Place peppers in food processor with garlic; pulse until finely chopped.

2. Add feta, yogurt, lemon juice and salt; pulse until well blended but still chunky. Serve with toast or vegetables. Store leftovers in airtight container in refrigerator up to 2 weeks.

Ratatouille

MAKES ABOUT 6 CUPS

2 tablespoons olive oil

1 medium onion, chopped

2 red bell peppers, cut into 1-inch pieces

3 cloves garlic, minced

1 teaspoon Italian seasoning

Pinch red pepper flakes

1 can (28 ounces) whole tomatoes, undrained, coarsely chopped or crushed with hands

1 medium eggplant (about 1 pound), cut into ½-inch pieces

3 small zucchini (about 12 ounces), cut in half lengthwise then cut crosswise into ¾-inch slices

1 fresh basil sprig

1 fresh rosemary sprig

1 tablespoon tomato paste

1½ teaspoons salt

¼ teaspoon black pepper

1 tablespoon balsamic or red wine vinegar

¼ cup chopped fresh basil

Toasted French bread slices

1. Heat oil in large saucepan or Dutch oven over medium-high heat. Add onion; cook and stir 2 minutes. Add bell peppers; cook and stir 3 minutes. Add garlic, Italian seasoning and red pepper flakes; cook and stir 30 seconds.

2. Stir in tomatoes with juice, eggplant, zucchini, basil sprig, rosemary sprig, tomato paste, salt and black pepper; mix well. Bring to a simmer. Reduce heat to medium-low; cover and simmer 30 minutes or until vegetables are tender and flavors are blended.

3. Remove and discard herb sprigs. Stir in vinegar and chopped basil. Serve warm or at room temperature with toast.

Zucchini Fritte

MAKES 4 SERVINGS

Lemon Aioli (recipe follows)

Vegetable oil for frying

¾ to 1 cup soda water

½ cup all-purpose flour

¼ cup cornstarch

½ teaspoon salt

¼ teaspoon garlic powder

¼ teaspoon dried oregano

¼ teaspoon black pepper

3 cups panko bread crumbs

1½ pounds medium zucchini (6 to 8 inches long), ends trimmed, cut lengthwise into ¼-inch-thick slices

¼ cup grated Parmesan or Romano cheese

Chopped fresh parsley

Lemon wedges

1. Prepare Lemon Aioli; cover and refrigerate until ready to serve.

2. Line baking sheet with paper towels; set aside. Pour oil into large saucepan or Dutch oven to depth of 2 inches; heat to 350°F over medium-high heat.

3. Meanwhile, pour ¾ cup soda water into large bowl. Combine flour, cornstarch, salt, garlic powder, oregano and pepper in small bowl; mix well. Slowly whisk flour mixture into soda water just until blended. Add additional soda water if necessary to reach consistency of thin pancake batter. Place panko in medium bowl.

4. Working with one at a time, dip zucchini slices into batter to coat; let excess batter drip back into bowl. Add to bowl with panko; press panko into zucchini slices to coat both sides completely. Place zucchini on prepared baking sheet.

5. Fry zucchini slices in batches 3 to 4 minutes or until golden brown. (Return oil to 350°F between batches.) Drain on paper towel-lined plate. Sprinkle with cheese and parsley; serve with Lemon Aioli and lemon wedges.

Lemon Aioli Combine ½ cup mayonnaise, 2 tablespoons lemon juice, 1 tablespoon finely chopped fresh parsley and 1 teaspoon minced garlic in small bowl; mix well. Season with salt and pepper.

Eggplant Parmesan Antipasti

MAKES 4 TO 6 SERVINGS

3 tablespoons olive oil, divided

1 clove garlic, minced

¼ teaspoon dried oregano

1 can (about 14 ounces) crushed tomatoes

¾ teaspoon salt, divided

6 fresh basil leaves, torn into small pieces

1 medium or 2 small eggplants* (about 1 pound)

½ teaspoon black pepper, divided

½ cup grated Parmesan cheese

4 to 6 ounces fresh mozzarella, cut into thin (⅛-inch) slices

Additional fresh basil leaves, chopped (optional)

Choose eggplant about 2½ to 3 inches in diameter to create smaller slices; avoid very large or bulbous eggplants.

1. Preheat broiler. Line large baking sheet with foil. Brush foil with 2 teaspoons oil.

2. Heat 1 tablespoon oil in medium saucepan over medium heat. Add garlic and oregano; cook and stir about 1 minute or just until fragrant. Add tomatoes and ¼ teaspoon salt; bring to a simmer. Simmer about 15 minutes; stir in basil.

3. Meanwhile, cut eggplant crosswise into ½-inch slices. Arrange eggplant on prepared baking sheet; brush with 2 teaspoons oil. Sprinkle with remaining ½ teaspoon salt and ¼ teaspoon pepper.

4. Broil 4 to 6 inches from heat source about 7 minutes or until well browned. Turn eggplant; brush with remaining 2 teaspoons oil and sprinkle with remaining ¼ teaspoon pepper. Broil about 6 minutes or until well browned.

5. Sprinkle each eggplant slice with 1 teaspoon Parmesan. Top with 1 tablespoon sauce, 1 mozzarella slice and 1 teaspoon Parmesan. Broil about 3 minutes or until cheese is bubbly and just beginning to brown. Sprinkle with chopped basil, if desired. Serve immediately.

Note There will be leftover tomato sauce after preparing this recipe; refrigerate or freeze leftovers.

Beans and Greens Crostini

MAKES ABOUT 24 CROSTINI

4 tablespoons olive oil, divided

1 small onion, thinly sliced

4 cups thinly sliced Italian black kale or other dinosaur kale variety

2 tablespoons minced garlic, divided

1 tablespoon balsamic vinegar

2 teaspoons salt, divided

¼ teaspoon red pepper flakes

1 can (about 15 ounces) cannellini beans, rinsed and drained

1 tablespoon chopped fresh rosemary

Toasted baguette slices

1. Heat 1 tablespoon oil in large skillet over medium heat. Add onion; cook and stir 5 minutes or until softened. Add kale and 1 tablespoon garlic; cook 15 minutes or until kale is softened and most liquid has evaporated, stirring occasionally. Stir in vinegar, 1 teaspoon salt and red pepper flakes.

2. Meanwhile, combine beans, remaining 3 tablespoons oil, 1 tablespoon garlic, 1 teaspoon salt and rosemary in food processor or blender; process until smooth.

3. Spread baguette slices with bean mixture; top with kale.

Tzatziki Dip

MAKES ABOUT 3 CUPS

1 cup finely diced peeled English cucumber

2 cups plain Greek yogurt

Grated peel and juice of 1 lemon

2 tablespoons minced fresh mint

2 tablespoons olive oil

1 tablespoon minced garlic

2 teaspoons salt

1½ teaspoons white wine vinegar

Grape tomatoes

Cut-up fresh vegetables: carrots, zucchini and/or bell pepper

1. Wrap cucumber in paper towel; squeeze to remove excess liquid. Place cucumber in medium bowl. Add yogurt, lemon peel, lemon juice, mint, oil, garlic, salt and vinegar; mix well. Cover and refrigerate at least 2 hours.

2. Place dip in serving bowl. Serve with vegetables.

Red Pepper Antipasto

MAKES 6 TO 8 SERVINGS

1 tablespoon olive oil

3 red bell peppers, cut into 2×¼-inch strips

2 cloves garlic, minced

2 tablespoons red wine vinegar

¼ teaspoon salt

Black pepper

1. Heat oil in large skillet over medium-high heat. Add bell peppers; cook and stir 8 to 9 minutes or until edges of peppers begin to brown. Reduce heat to medium. Add garlic; cook and stir 1 minute.

2. Add vinegar, salt and black pepper; cook 2 minutes or until liquid has evaporated. Serve warm or at room temperature.

Red Pepper Crostini Brush thin slices of French bread with olive oil. Place on baking sheet; bake in preheated 350°F oven 10 minutes or until crisp and golden brown. Top with Red Pepper Antipasto.

Simple Bruschetta

MAKES 4 SERVINGS

1 tablespoon olive oil

2 tablespoons thinly sliced red onion

1 clove garlic, minced

1 cup chopped seeded tomatoes

¼ teaspoon salt

⅛ teaspoon black pepper

8 thin baguette slices, toasted or grilled

¼ cup slivered fresh basil

1. Heat oil in medium skillet over medium heat. Add onion; cook and stir 3 minutes or until softened. Add garlic; cook and stir 1 minute.

2. Stir in tomatoes, salt and pepper; let stand 10 minutes. Serve mixture on toast; sprinkle with basil.

Roasted Vegetable Spread

MAKES ABOUT 2 CUPS

1 zucchini, cut into 1-inch cubes

1 yellow squash, cut into 1-inch cubes

1 red bell pepper, cut into 1-inch cubes

1 red onion, thinly sliced

2 carrots, chopped

2 cloves garlic, peeled and smashed

2 tablespoons olive oil

1 teaspoon salt

½ teaspoon black pepper

1 tablespoon lemon juice

Pita chips

1. Preheat oven to 425°F.

2. Place vegetables on large baking sheet. Drizzle with oil; sprinkle with salt and pepper. Toss to coat; spread in single layer on baking sheet. Roast 30 to 40 minutes or until vegetables are soft and browned. Cool slightly on baking sheet.

3. Place vegetables in food processor with lemon juice. Process 1 minute or until mixture is smooth. Serve with pita chips.

Mediterranean Baked Feta

MAKES 4 TO 6 SERVINGS

1 block (8 ounces) feta cheese, cut crosswise into 4 slices

½ cup grape tomatoes, halved

¼ cup sliced roasted red peppers

¼ cup pitted Kalamata olives

⅛ teaspoon dried oregano

Black pepper

2 tablespoons olive oil

1 tablespoon shredded fresh basil

Pita chips

1. Preheat oven to 400°F.

2. Place cheese in small baking dish; top with tomatoes, roasted peppers and olives. Sprinkle with oregano and season with black pepper; drizzle with oil.

3. Bake 12 minutes or until cheese is soft. Sprinkle with basil. Serve immediately with pita chips.

Roasted Eggplant Hummus

MAKES ABOUT 1½ CUPS

1 large eggplant (about 1½ pounds)

¼ cup tahini

2 tablespoons lemon juice

1 clove garlic

Salt and black pepper

Pita bread wedges

1. Preheat oven to 400°F. Line small baking sheet with foil.

2. Place eggplant on baking sheet; roast about 1 hour or until soft. When cool enough to handle, remove and discard skin.

3. Combine eggplant, tahini, lemon juice and garlic in food processor; process until smooth. Season with salt and pepper to taste. Serve with pita.

Pissaladière
(French-Style Pizza Bites)

MAKES ABOUT 24 SERVINGS

2 tablespoons olive oil

1 medium onion, thinly sliced

1 medium red bell pepper, cut into 3-inch-long strips

2 cloves garlic, minced

⅓ cup pitted black olives, cut into thin wedges

1 ball (about 16 ounces) refrigerated pizza dough

¾ cup (3 ounces) finely shredded Swiss or Gruyère cheese

1. Preheat oven to 425°F. Grease large baking sheet.

2. Heat oil in medium skillet over medium heat. Add onion, bell pepper and garlic; cook and stir 5 minutes or until crisp-tender. Stir in olives. Remove from heat.

3. Using greased or floured hands, pat dough into 16×12-inch rectangle on prepared baking sheet. Arrange onion mixture over dough; sprinkle with cheese. Bake 10 minutes. Loosen crust with long spatula; slide onto oven rack. Bake 3 to 5 minutes more or until golden brown.

4. Slide baking sheet under crust and remove crust from rack. Transfer to cutting board. Cut pizza crosswise into eight 1¾-inch-wide strips; cut diagonally into ten 2-inch-wide strips, making diamond pieces. Serve immediately.

Orzo Spinach Pie

MAKES 8 SERVINGS

⅔ cup uncooked orzo

1 cup milk

3 eggs

¼ teaspoon salt

⅛ teaspoon ground nutmeg

⅛ teaspoon black pepper

1 package (10 ounces) frozen chopped spinach, thawed and squeezed dry

4 tablespoons grated Parmesan cheese, divided

¾ cup fresh whole wheat bread crumbs*

1 tablespoon butter, melted

To make fresh bread crumbs, tear 1½ slices bread into pieces; process in food processor until coarse crumbs form.

1. Preheat oven to 375°F. Spray 9-inch pie plate with nonstick cooking spray.

2. Cook orzo in large saucepan of salted boiling water according to package directions for al dente. Drain.

3. Whisk milk, eggs, salt, nutmeg and pepper in large bowl until well blended. Stir in spinach and 2 tablespoons cheese. Add orzo; mix gently. Spoon evenly into prepared pie plate. Combine bread crumbs and remaining 2 tablespoons cheese in small bowl. Stir in butter. Sprinkle evenly over spinach mixture.

4. Bake 20 minutes or until topping is golden brown and center is set. Let stand 5 minutes. Cut into wedges to serve.

Kashk-E Bademjan
(Persian Eggplant Dip)

MAKES 12 TO 16 SERVINGS

3 large eggplants (3½ pounds total), peeled and cut into 1-inch cubes

1 teaspoon salt

5 tablespoons olive oil, divided

2 onions, chopped

1 tablespoon dried mint

3 tablespoons plain Greek yogurt

⅓ cup finely chopped walnuts

Pita bread and/or assorted vegetable sticks

Slow Cooker Recipes

1. Toss eggplant cubes with salt in large bowl; transfer to large colander. Place colander in large bowl or sink; let stand 1 hour at room temperature to drain.

2. Meanwhile, heat 1 tablespoon oil in large nonstick skillet over medium-high heat. Add onions; cook 5 to 6 minutes or until lightly browned, stirring occasionally. Transfer to slow cooker. Stir in eggplant. Cover; cook on LOW 6 to 8 hours or on HIGH 3½ to 4 hours or until eggplant is very soft.

3. Heat remaining 4 tablespoons oil in small saucepan over low heat. Add mint; cook about 15 minutes or until very fragrant. Set aside to cool slightly.

4. Transfer eggplant and onions to colander or fine mesh strainer with slotted spoon; press out any excess liquid with back of spoon. Return to slow cooker; mash with fork. Stir in yogurt. Sprinkle with chopped walnuts; drizzle with mint oil. Serve warm with pita bread and/or assorted vegetable sticks.

Note Make this dip ahead of time on a weekend and enjoy it all week long.

Soups & Salads

Fresh Tomato Pasta Soup

MAKES 8 SERVINGS

1 tablespoon olive oil

½ cup chopped onion

1 clove garlic, minced

3 pounds fresh tomatoes (about 9 medium), coarsely chopped

3 cups vegetable broth

1 tablespoon minced fresh basil

1 tablespoon minced fresh marjoram

1 tablespoon minced fresh oregano

1 teaspoon whole fennel seeds

½ teaspoon black pepper

¾ cup uncooked rosamarina, orzo or other small pasta

½ cup (2 ounces) shredded mozzarella cheese

1. Heat oil in large saucepan over medium heat. Add onion and garlic; cook and stir 5 minutes or until onion is tender.

2. Add tomatoes, broth, basil, marjoram, oregano, fennel seeds and pepper; bring to a boil. Reduce heat to low; cover and simmer 25 minutes. Remove from heat; cool slightly.

3. Purée tomato mixture in batches in food processor or blender (or use immersion blender). Return to saucepan; bring to a boil. Add pasta; cook 7 to 9 minutes or until tender. Sprinkle with cheese.

Italian Crouton Salad

MAKES 6 SERVINGS

6 ounces French or Italian bread

¼ cup plain yogurt

¼ cup red wine vinegar

2 tablespoons olive oil

3 cloves garlic, minced

6 medium plum tomatoes, sliced (about 3¾ to 4 cups)

½ medium red onion, thinly sliced

3 tablespoons sliced fresh basil

2 tablespoons finely chopped fresh parsley

12 leaves red leaf lettuce *or* 4 cups prepared Italian salad mix

2 tablespoons grated Parmesan cheese

1. Preheat broiler. For croutons, cut bread into ¾-inch cubes. Place in single layer on baking sheet. Broil 4 inches from heat source 3 minutes or until bread is golden, stirring every 30 seconds to 1 minute. Place croutons in large bowl.

2. Whisk yogurt, vinegar, oil and garlic in small bowl until blended. Add tomatoes, onion, basil and parsley to croutons; stir to combine. Pour yogurt mixture over salad; toss to coat. Cover; refrigerate 30 minutes or up to 1 day. (Croutons will be softer the following day.)

3. Serve salad on lettuce leaves; sprinkle with cheese.

Minestrone Soup

MAKES 4 TO 6 SERVINGS

1 tablespoon olive oil

1 onion, chopped

1 stalk celery, diced

1 carrot, diced

2 cloves garlic, minced

4 cups vegetable broth or water

1 bay leaf

¾ teaspoon salt

½ teaspoon dried basil

½ teaspoon dried oregano

¼ teaspoon dried thyme

¼ teaspoon sugar

¼ teaspoon black pepper

1 can (about 15 ounces) dark red kidney beans, rinsed and drained

1 can (about 15 ounces) navy beans or cannellini beans, rinsed and drained

1 can (about 14 ounces) diced tomatoes

1 cup diced zucchini (about 1 small)

½ cup uncooked small shell pasta

½ cup fresh or frozen cut green beans

¼ cup dry red wine *or* 1 tablespoon balsamic vinegar

1 cup packed chopped fresh spinach

Grated Parmesan cheese (optional)

1. Heat oil in large saucepan or Dutch oven over medium-high heat. Add onion, celery, carrot and garlic; cook and stir 5 to 7 minutes or until vegetables are tender. Add broth, bay leaf, salt, basil, oregano, thyme, sugar and pepper; bring to a boil.

2. Stir in beans, tomatoes, zucchini, pasta, green beans and wine; cook 10 minutes, stirring occasionally.

3. Add spinach; cook 2 minutes or until pasta and zucchini are tender. Remove and discard bay leaf.

Greek Salad

MAKES 6 SERVINGS

Salad

- 3 medium tomatoes, cut into 8 wedges each
- 1 green bell pepper, cut into 1-inch pieces
- ½ English cucumber (8 to 10 inches), quartered lengthwise and sliced crosswise
- ½ red onion, thinly sliced
- ½ cup pitted Kalamata olives
- 1 block (8 ounces) feta cheese, cut into ½-inch cubes

Dressing

- 6 tablespoons olive oil
- 3 tablespoons red wine vinegar
- 1 to 2 cloves garlic, minced
- ¾ teaspoon dried oregano
- ¾ teaspoon salt
- ¼ teaspoon black pepper

1. For salad, combine tomatoes, bell pepper, cucumber, onion and olives in large bowl. Top with feta.

2. For dressing, whisk oil, vinegar, garlic, oregano, salt and black pepper in small bowl until well blended. Pour over salad; stir gently to coat.

Fasolada
(Greek White Bean Soup)

MAKES 4 TO 6 SERVINGS

4 tablespoons olive oil, divided

1 large onion, diced

3 stalks celery, diced

3 carrots, diced

4 cloves garlic, minced

¼ cup tomato paste

1 teaspoon salt

1 teaspoon dried oregano

½ teaspoon ground cumin

¼ teaspoon black pepper

1 bay leaf

4 cups vegetable broth

3 cans (15 ounces each) cannellini beans, rinsed and drained

2 tablespoons lemon juice

¼ cup minced fresh parsley

1. Heat 2 tablespoons oil in large saucepan over medium-high heat. Add onion, celery and carrots; cook and stir 8 to 10 minutes or until vegetables are softened. Stir in garlic; cook and stir 30 seconds. Stir in tomato paste, salt, oregano, cumin, pepper and bay leaf; cook and stir 30 seconds.

2. Stir in broth; bring to a boil. Stir in beans; return to a boil. Reduce heat to medium-low; simmer 30 minutes. Stir in remaining 2 tablespoons oil and lemon juice. Remove and discard bay leaf. Sprinkle with parsley just before serving.

Zucchini Chickpea Salad

MAKES 4 TO 6 SERVINGS

3 medium zucchini

½ teaspoon salt

5 tablespoons white vinegar

1 clove garlic, minced

¼ teaspoon dried thyme

½ cup olive oil

1 can (about 15 ounces) chickpeas, rinsed and drained

½ cup sliced pitted black olives

3 green onions, minced

1 ripe avocado, cut into ½-inch cubes

⅓ cup crumbled feta cheese

1 canned chipotle pepper in adobo sauce, seeded and minced

Boston lettuce leaves and sliced fresh tomatoes (optional)

1. Cut zucchini lengthwise into halves; cut halves crosswise into ¼-inch-thick slices. Place in medium bowl; sprinkle with salt. Toss to mix. Spread zucchini on several layers of paper towels. Let stand at room temperature 30 minutes to drain.

2. Combine vinegar, garlic and thyme in large bowl. Gradually whisk in oil until well blended. Pat zucchini dry; add to dressing. Add chickpeas, olives and onions; toss to coat. Cover and refrigerate at least 30 minutes or up to 4 hours, stirring occasionally.

3. Stir in avocado, cheese and chipotle pepper before serving. If desired, line shallow bowls or small plates with lettuce leaves and tomato slices. Top with salad.

Roasted Vegetable Salad with Capers and Walnuts

MAKES 6 TO 8 SERVINGS

1 pound small Brussels sprouts, trimmed

1 pound small Yukon Gold potatoes, halved

5 tablespoons olive oil, divided

½ teaspoon salt

¼ teaspoon black pepper

¼ teaspoon dried rosemary

1 red bell pepper, cut into bite-size pieces

¼ cup walnuts, coarsely chopped

2 tablespoons capers, drained

1½ tablespoons white wine vinegar

1. Preheat oven to 400°F.

2. Cut an X into stem ends of Brussels sprouts; place in shallow roasting pan or baking sheet. Add potatoes. Drizzle with 3 tablespoons oil and sprinkle with salt, black pepper and rosemary; toss to coat. Spread vegetables in single layer in pan.

3. Roast vegetables 20 minutes. Stir in bell pepper; roast 15 minutes or until tender. Remove to large bowl; stir in walnuts and capers.

4. Whisk remaining 2 tablespoons oil and vinegar in small bowl until well blended. Pour over salad; toss to coat. Serve at room temperature.

Greek Lemon and Rice Soup

MAKES 6 TO 8 SERVINGS

2 **tablespoons butter**

⅓ **cup minced green onions**

6 **cups vegetable or chicken broth**

⅔ **cup uncooked long grain rice**

½ **teaspoon salt**

4 **eggs**

Juice of 1 lemon

⅛ **teaspoon black or white pepper**

1. Melt butter in medium saucepan over medium heat. Add green onions; cook and stir 3 minutes or until tender.

2. Stir in broth, rice and salt; bring to a boil over medium-high heat. Reduce heat to low; cover and simmer 20 to 25 minutes or until rice is tender.

3. Beat eggs in medium bowl. Stir in lemon juice and ½ cup hot broth mixture until blended. Gradually pour egg mixture into broth mixture in saucepan, stirring constantly. Cook and stir over low heat 2 to 3 minutes or until soup thickens enough to lightly coat spoon. *Do not boil.* Stir in pepper.

Greek-Style Chicken Stew

MAKES 6 SERVINGS

3 pounds bone-in chicken breasts, skin removed

All-purpose flour

3 tablespoons olive oil

2 cups cubed peeled eggplant

2 cups sliced mushrooms

1 medium onion, chopped

2 cloves garlic, minced

1 teaspoon dried oregano

½ teaspoon dried basil

½ teaspoon dried thyme

2 cups chicken broth

¼ cup dry sherry or additional chicken broth

¼ teaspoon salt

¼ teaspoon black pepper

1 can (14 ounces) artichoke hearts, drained and halved

3 cups hot cooked wide egg noodles

1. Coat chicken lightly with flour. Heat oil in Dutch oven or large saucepan over medium heat. Add chicken; cook 10 to 15 minutes or until browned on all sides. Remove chicken to plate.

2. Add eggplant, mushrooms, onion, garlic, oregano, basil and thyme to Dutch oven; cook over medium heat 5 minutes, scraping up browned bits from bottom of pot.

3. Return chicken to Dutch oven. Stir in broth, sherry, salt and pepper; bring to a boil. Reduce heat to low; cover and simmer 1 hour or until chicken is cooked through (165°F). Add artichokes during last 20 minutes of cooking. Serve over noodles.

Greek Lentil Salad with Feta Vinaigrette

MAKES 4 SERVINGS

4 cups water

1 cup uncooked lentils

1½ teaspoons salt, divided

1 bay leaf

¼ cup chopped green onions

1 large stalk celery, chopped

1 cup grape tomatoes, halved

¼ cup (1 ounce) crumbled feta cheese

2 tablespoons olive oil

1 tablespoon white wine vinegar

½ teaspoon dried thyme

½ teaspoon dried oregano

¼ teaspoon black pepper

1. Combine water, lentils, 1 teaspoon salt and bay leaf in small saucepan. Bring to a boil. Reduce heat to medium-low; partially cover and cook 20 to 25 minutes or until lentils are tender but not mushy.

2. Drain lentils; remove and discard bay leaf. Place lentils in serving bowl; stir in green onions, celery and tomatoes.

3. Combine feta, oil, vinegar, thyme, oregano, remaining ½ teaspoon salt and pepper in small bowl. Pour over salad; gently stir until blended. Let stand at least 10 minutes before serving to allow flavors to blend.

Pasta Fagioli Soup

MAKES 4 TO 6 SERVINGS

1 tablespoon olive oil

1 onion, finely chopped

2 zucchini, quartered lengthwise and sliced

2 teaspoons minced garlic

3½ cups vegetable broth

1 can (about 15 ounces) Great Northern beans, rinsed and drained

1 can (about 14 ounces) diced tomatoes

½ teaspoon dried basil

½ teaspoon dried oregano

½ teaspoon salt

¼ teaspoon black pepper

½ cup uncooked tubetti, ditalini or small shell pasta

½ cup croutons or toasted bread cubes

½ cup grated Asiago or Romano cheese

Chopped fresh parsley (optional)

1. Heat oil in large saucepan over medium-high heat. Add onion and zucchini; cook and stir 5 minutes or until onion is softened. Add garlic; cook and stir 5 minutes or until onion is softened.

2. Add broth, beans, tomatoes, basil, oregano, salt and pepper; bring to a boil. Reduce heat to medium; simmer 30 minutes. Add pasta; cook about 10 minutes or until pasta is tender.

3. Serve soup with croutons, cheese and parsley.

Middle Eastern Lentil Soup

MAKES 4 SERVINGS

2 tablespoons olive oil

1 small onion, chopped

1 red bell pepper, chopped

1 teaspoon whole fennel seeds

½ teaspoon ground cumin

¼ teaspoon ground red pepper

4 cups water

1 cup dried lentils, rinsed and sorted

½ teaspoon salt

1 tablespoon lemon juice

½ cup plain Greek yogurt

2 tablespoons chopped fresh parsley

1. Heat oil in large saucepan over medium-high heat. Add onion and bell pepper; cook and stir 5 minutes or until tender. Add fennel seeds, cumin and red pepper; cook and stir 1 minute.

2. Add water, lentils and salt; bring to a boil. Reduce heat to low; cover and simmer 25 to 30 minutes or until lentils are tender. Stir in lemon juice.

3. Top each serving with yogurt; sprinkle with parsley.

Lentil and Orzo Pasta Salad

MAKES 4 SERVINGS

8 cups water

1 teaspoon salt

½ cup dried lentils, rinsed and sorted

4 ounces uncooked orzo pasta

1½ cups quartered cherry tomatoes

¾ cup finely chopped celery

½ cup chopped red onion

2 ounces pitted olives (about 16 olives), coarsely chopped

3 to 4 tablespoons cider vinegar

1 tablespoon olive oil

1 teaspoon dried basil

1 clove garlic, minced

⅛ teaspoon red pepper flakes

4 ounces crumbled feta cheese with sun-dried tomatoes and basil

Salt and black pepper (optional)

1. Bring water and 1 teaspoon salt to a boil in large saucepan. Add lentils; cook 12 minutes.

2. Add orzo; cook 10 minutes or just until orzo and lentils are tender. Drain and rinse under cold water until cool.

3. Meanwhile, combine tomatoes, celery, onion, olives, vinegar, oil, basil, garlic and red pepper flakes in large bowl; mix well.

4. Add lentil mixture to tomato mixture; toss gently to blend. Add cheese; toss gently. Let stand 15 minutes before serving. Season with salt and pepper, if desired.

Peppery Sicilian Chicken Soup

MAKES 8 TO 10 SERVINGS

2 tablespoons olive oil

1 onion, chopped

1 green bell pepper, chopped

3 stalks celery, chopped

3 carrots, chopped

3 cloves garlic, minced

1 tablespoon salt

3 containers (32 ounces each) chicken broth

2 pounds boneless skinless chicken breasts

1 can (28 ounces) diced tomatoes

2 baking potatoes, peeled and cut into ¼-inch pieces

1½ teaspoons ground white pepper*

1½ teaspoons ground black pepper

½ cup chopped fresh parsley

8 ounces uncooked ditalini pasta

Or substitute additional black pepper for the white pepper.

1. Heat oil in large saucepan or Dutch oven over medium heat. Add onion, bell pepper, celery and carrots. Reduce heat to medium-low; cover and cook 10 to 15 minutes or until vegetables are tender but not browned, stirring occasionally. Stir in garlic and 1 tablespoon salt; cover and cook 5 minutes.

2. Stir in broth, chicken, tomatoes, potatoes, white pepper and black pepper; bring to a boil. Reduce heat to low; cover and simmer 1 hour. Remove chicken to plate; set aside until cool enough to handle. Shred chicken and return to saucepan with parsley.

3. Meanwhile, cook pasta in medium saucepan of salted boiling water 7 minutes (or 1 minute less than package directs for al dente). Drain pasta and add to soup. Taste and season with additional salt, if desired.

Sandwiches & Breads

Mediterranean Vegetable Sandwich

MAKES 4 SANDWICHES

½ cup plain hummus

½ jalapeño pepper, seeded and minced

¼ cup minced fresh cilantro

8 slices whole wheat bread

4 leaves lettuce (leaf or Bibb lettuce)

2 tomatoes, thinly sliced

½ cucumber, thinly sliced

½ red onion, thinly sliced

½ cup thinly sliced peppadew peppers or sweet Italian peppers

4 tablespoons (1 ounce) crumbled feta cheese

1. Combine hummus, jalapeño and cilantro in small bowl; mix well.

2. Spread about 1 tablespoon hummus mixture on one side of each bread slice. Layer half of bread slices with lettuce, tomatoes, cucumber, onion, peppadew peppers and feta; top with remaining bread slices. Serve immediately.

Tomato Mozzarella Sandwich

MAKES 4 SERVINGS

Balsamic Vinaigrette

- 6 tablespoons olive oil
- 3 tablespoons balsamic vinegar
- 1 clove garlic, minced
- 1 teaspoon honey
- 1 teaspoon Dijon mustard
- ½ teaspoon dried oregano
- ½ teaspoon salt
- ⅛ teaspoon black pepper

Sandwiches

- 1 baguette (1 pound), ends trimmed, cut into 4 equal pieces and split
- 1 cup loosely packed baby arugula
- 3 medium tomatoes, sliced ¼ inch thick
- 1 cup roasted red peppers, patted dry and thinly sliced
- 12 slices fresh mozzarella (one 8-ounce package)
- 12 fresh basil leaves

1. For vinaigrette, whisk oil, vinegar, garlic, honey, mustard, oregano, salt and black pepper in small bowl until well blended.

2. For each sandwich, drizzle 1 tablespoon vinaigrette over bottom half of bread. Layer with arugula, tomatoes, roasted peppers, cheese, additional arugula and basil. Drizzle with 1 tablespoon vinaigrette; replace top half of bread.

Chicken Pesto Flatbreads

MAKES 2 SERVINGS

2 tablespoons prepared pesto

2 (6- to 7-inch) round flatbreads or Greek-style pita bread rounds (no pocket)

1 cup grilled chicken strips

4 slices (1 ounce each) mozzarella cheese

1 plum tomato, cut into ¼-inch slices

3 tablespoons shredded Parmesan cheese

1. Spread 1 tablespoon pesto over half of each flatbread. Place chicken on opposite half of bread; top with mozzarella, tomato and Parmesan. Fold pesto-topped bread half over filling.

2. Spray grill pan or nonstick skillet with nonstick cooking spray or brush with vegetable oil; heat over medium-high heat. Cook sandwiches 3 minutes per side or until bread is toasted, cheese begins to melt and sandwiches are heated through.

Whole Wheat Focaccia

MAKES 8 SERVINGS

2 cups all-purpose flour

1¾ cups whole wheat flour

3 teaspoons Italian seasoning, divided

1 package (¼ ounce) active dry yeast (2¼ teaspoons)

1 teaspoon salt

1½ cups warm water (120°F)

3 tablespoons olive oil, divided

¼ cup shredded Parmesan cheese

1. Combine all-purpose flour, whole wheat flour, 1½ teaspoons Italian seasoning, yeast and salt in large bowl. Make well in center; stir in water and 1 tablespoon oil until soft, sticky dough forms. Or mix with electric mixer at medium-low speed until dough forms.

2. Place remaining 2 tablespoons oil in 13×9-inch baking pan. Place dough in pan; turn to coat with oil. Pat and stretch dough to edges of pan. Cover and let rise in warm place 1 hour or until doubled in size.

3. Preheat oven 400°F. Dimple top of dough with fingertips; sprinkle with remaining 1½ teaspoons seasoning and cheese.

4. Bake 18 to 20 minutes or until top is golden brown and bread sounds hollow when tapped. Remove from pan; cool on wire rack. Cut into squares to serve.

Turkey Mozzarella Panini

MAKES 2 TO 4 SERVINGS

Bacon Jam

- 1 pound thick-cut bacon, chopped
- 2 large onions, chopped (about 1 pound)
- ⅓ cup packed brown sugar
- ⅛ teaspoon red pepper flakes
- ⅔ cup water
- ¼ cup coffee
- 1½ tablespoons balsamic vinegar

Garlic Aioli

- ¼ cup mayonnaise
- 1 clove garlic, minced
- 1 teaspoon lemon juice
- ⅛ teaspoon salt

Panini

- 2 (6- to 7-inch) round focaccia breads, split
- 2 plum tomatoes, cut into ¼-inch slices
- 6 ounces sliced fresh mozzarella (¼-inch-thick slices)
- 6 ounces thickly sliced turkey breast (about ¼-inch-thick slices)
- ½ cup baby arugula

1. For bacon jam, cook bacon in large skillet over medium-high heat 10 to 15 minutes or until bacon is cooked through but still chewy (not crisp), stirring occasionally. Remove bacon to paper towel-lined plate. Drain off all but 1 tablespoon drippings from skillet.

2. Add onions to skillet; cook 10 minutes, stirring occasionally. Add brown sugar and red pepper flakes; cook over medium-low heat 18 to 20 minutes or until onions are deep golden brown. Stir in bacon, water and coffee; cook over medium heat 25 minutes or until mixture is thick and jammy, stirring occasionally. Stir in vinegar.*

3. For garlic aioli, combine mayonnaise, garlic, lemon juice and salt in small bowl; mix well.

4. Spread bottom halves of focaccia with garlic aioli. Top with tomatoes, cheese, turkey and arugula. Spread top halves of focaccia with bacon jam; place over arugula. Serve immediately.

Recipe makes about 1½ cups bacon jam. Store remaining jam in refrigerator up to 2 weeks; return to room temperature before serving.

Quattro Formaggio Focaccia

MAKES 12 TO 15 SERVINGS

1 tablespoon sugar

1 package (¼ ounce) instant yeast (2¼ teaspoons)

1¼ cups warm water (100° to 105°F)

3 to 3¼ cups all-purpose flour

¼ cup plus 2 tablespoons olive oil, divided

1 teaspoon salt

¼ cup marinara sauce with basil

1 cup (4 ounces) shredded Italian cheese blend

1. Dissolve sugar and yeast in warm water in large bowl of stand mixer; let stand 5 minutes or until bubbly. Stir in 3 cups flour, ¼ cup oil and salt with spoon or spatula to form rough dough. Mix with dough hook at low speed 5 minutes, adding additional flour, 1 tablespoon at a time, if necessary for dough to come together. (Dough will be sticky and will not clean side of bowl.)

2. Shape dough into a ball. Place dough in large greased bowl; turn to grease top. Cover and let rise 1 to 1½ hours or until doubled in size.

3. Punch down dough. Pour remaining 2 tablespoons oil into 13×9-inch baking pan; pat and stretch dough to fill pan. Make indentations in top of dough with fingertips.

4. Spread marinara sauce evenly over dough; sprinkle with cheese. Cover and let rise 30 minutes or until puffy. Preheat oven to 425°F.

5. Bake 17 to 20 minutes or until golden brown. Remove from pan to wire rack or cutting board. Cut into squares or strips.

Khachapuri
(Georgian Cheese Bread)

MAKES 2 SERVINGS

1 loaf (16 ounces) frozen bread dough, thawed according to package directions

1½ cups (6 ounces) shredded mozzarella cheese

1½ cups (6 ounces) crumbled feta cheese

1 teaspoon olive oil

1 teaspoon everything bagel seasoning (optional)

2 eggs

Black pepper

1. Line baking sheet with parchment paper. Divide dough in half. Roll out one half into 11×8½-inch oval on lightly floured surface; remove to prepared baking sheet.

2. Combine mozzarella and feta in medium bowl; mix well. Sprinkle ½ cup cheese mixture over dough, spreading almost to edge. Starting with long sides of oval, roll up dough and cheese towards center, curving into boat shape and leaving about 3 inches open in center. Press ends to seal. Fill center with 1 cup cheese mixture. Repeat with remaining dough and cheese mixture.

3. Cover loosely with plastic wrap; let rise 20 to 30 minutes or until puffy. Preheat oven to 400°F. Just before baking, brush edges of dough with oil; sprinkle with everything bagel seasoning, if desired.

4. Bake 12 minutes. Remove baking sheet from oven; use back of spoon to create indentations for eggs in center of cheese. Crack egg into each indentation;* sprinkle with pepper.

5. Bake 8 minutes for soft eggs; bake 10 minutes for firm eggs. Serve warm.

For more control, crack egg into small bowl and slide egg from bowl into cheese mixture.

Open-Faced Lamb Naan Sandwiches with Raita

MAKES 4 SERVINGS

1 tablespoon olive oil

1 red onion, diced

1 pound ground lamb

1 tablespoon tomato paste

1¼ teaspoons minced garlic, divided

1 teaspoon ground cumin

½ teaspoon ground corinader

1¼ teaspoons salt, divided

¼ cup diced English cucumber

¾ cup plain Greek yogurt

2 tablespoons chopped fresh cilantro

4 pieces naan bread, lightly toasted

1. Heat oil in large skillet over medium heat. Add onion; cook 5 minutes or until softened. Transfer to small bowl.

2. Add lamb to same skillet; cook over medium-high heat about 8 minutes or until browned, stirring occasionally. Add tomato paste, 1 teaspoon garlic, cumin, coriander and 1 teaspoon salt; cook 1 minute, stirring constantly. Add onion; cook 1 minute.

3. For raita, combine cucumber, yogurt, remaining ¼ teaspoon garlic, cilantro and remaining ¼ teaspoon salt in medium bowl.

4. Divide lamb evenly among naan; top with raita. Serve immediately.

Spanikopita Pull-Aparts

MAKES 24 ROLLS

4 tablespoons (½ stick) butter, melted, divided

12 frozen white dinner rolls (⅓ of 3-pound package),* thawed according to package directions

1 package (10 ounces) frozen chopped spinach, thawed and squeezed dry

4 green onions, finely chopped (about ¼ cup packed)

1 clove garlic, minced

1 teaspoon dried dill weed

½ teaspoon salt

⅛ teaspoon black pepper

1 cup (4 ounces) crumbled feta cheese

¾ cup (3 ounces) grated Monterey Jack cheese, divided

If frozen dinner rolls are not available, substitute one 16-ounce loaf of frozen bread dough or pizza dough. Thaw according to package directions and divide into 12 pieces.

1. Brush large (10-inch) ovenproof skillet with ½ tablespoon butter. Cut rolls in half to make 24 balls of dough.

2. Combine spinach, green onions, garlic, dill, salt and pepper in medium bowl; mix well to break apart spinach. Add feta, ½ cup Monterey Jack and remaining 3½ tablespoons butter; mix well.

3. Coat each ball of dough with spinach mixture; arrange in single layer in prepared skillet. Sprinkle any remaining spinach mixture between and over balls of dough. Cover and let rise in warm place about 40 minutes or until almost doubled in size. Preheat oven to 350°F. Sprinkle remaining ¼ cup Monterey Jack over dough.

4. Bake 35 to 40 minutes or until golden brown. Serve warm.

Red Pepper and Olive Focaccia

MAKES 12 SERVINGS

1 package (¼ ounce) active dry yeast (2¼ teaspoons)

1 teaspoon sugar

1½ cups warm water (105° to 115°F)

4 cups all-purpose flour, divided

7 tablespoons olive oil, divided

1 teaspoon salt

¼ cup bottled roasted red peppers, drained and cut into strips

¼ cup pitted black olives

1. Dissolve yeast and sugar in warm water in large bowl of stand mixer; let stand 5 minutes or until bubbly. Add 3½ cups flour, 3 tablespoons oil and salt; mix with dough hook at low speed until soft dough forms. Add remaining flour, 1 tablespoon at a time, if necessary to prevent sticking. Knead 5 minutes or until dough is smooth and elastic.

2. Shape dough into a ball. Place dough in greased bowl; turn to grease top. Cover and let rise in warm place 1 hour or until doubled in size.

3. Brush 15×10-inch baking pan with 1 tablespoon oil. Punch down dough; turn out onto lightly floured surface. Flatten dough into rectangle; roll out almost to size of pan. Place dough in pan; gently press dough to edges.

4. Make indentations in top of dough every 1 or 2 inches with fingertips or handle of wooden spoon. Brush with remaining 3 tablespoons oil. Gently press roasted peppers and olives into dough. Cover and let rise in warm place 30 minutes or until doubled in size. Preheat oven to 450°F.

5. Bake 12 to 18 minutes or until golden brown. Cut into squares or rectangles. Serve warm.

Olive Herb Pull-Aparts

MAKES 10 SERVINGS

3 tablespoons olive oil, divided

4 cloves garlic, minced

1 package (12 ounces) refrigerated buttermilk biscuits (10 biscuits) *or* 10 frozen dinner rolls, thawed according to package directions

¼ teaspoon red pepper flakes

1 red onion, very thinly sliced

½ cup shredded or chopped fresh basil

½ (2¼-ounce) can sliced black olives, drained

2 teaspoons chopped fresh rosemary

¼ cup (1 ounce) crumbled feta cheese

1. Preheat oven to 400°F. Line large baking sheet with parchment paper or spray with nonstick cooking spray.

2. Combine 1 tablespoon oil and garlic in small bowl. Separate biscuits; arrange on baking sheet about ½ inch apart. Brush with 1 tablespoon oil; let stand 10 minutes.

3. Flatten biscuits. Sprinkle with red pepper flakes, gently pressing into biscuits. Brush with garlic oil; top with onion.

4. Combine basil, olives, rosemary and remaining 1 tablespoon oil in small bowl. Spread mixture over biscuits; sprinkle with feta.

5. Bake 10 minutes or until golden brown (15 minutes for dinner rolls). Serve warm or at room temperature.

Greek Chicken Pitas
with Creamy Mustard Sauce

MAKES 4 SERVINGS

2 tablespoons olive oil, divided

1 green bell pepper, cut into ½-inch strips

1 onion, cut into 8 wedges

1 pound boneless skinless chicken breasts, pounded to ½-inch thickness

2 teaspoons Greek seasoning

¾ teaspoon salt, divided

¼ cup plain Greek yogurt

¼ cup mayonnaise

1 tablespoon prepared mustard

4 pita bread rounds

½ cup crumbled feta cheese

Optional toppings: sliced cucumbers, sliced tomatoes and/or kalamata olives

1. Heat 1 tablespoon oil in large skillet over medium-high heat. Add bell peppers and onion; cook and stir 5 minutes or until softened. Transfer to plate.

2. Sprinkle chicken with seasoning and ½ teaspoon salt. Heat remaining 1 tablespoon oil in same skillet. Add chicken; cook 10 minutes or until chicken is browned and cooked though (165°F), turning once. Transfer chicken to cutting board; cut into slices.

3. Combine yogurt, mayonnaise, mustard and remaining ¼ teaspoon salt in small bowl; stir until blended.

4. Warm pitas according to package directions. Cut in half and fill pockets with chicken, mustard sauce, vegetables, cheese and desired toppings.

Grilled Italian Chicken Panini

MAKES 6 SERVINGS

6 small portobello mushroom caps (about 6 ounces)

½ cup plus 2 tablespoons balsamic vinaigrette

1 loaf (16 ounces) Italian bread, cut into 12 slices

12 slices provolone cheese

1½ cups chopped cooked chicken

1 jar (12 ounces) roasted red peppers, drained

1. Brush mushrooms with 2 tablespoons vinaigrette. Cook mushrooms in large nonstick skillet over medium-high heat 5 to 7 minutes or until softened. Cut diagonally into ½-inch slices.

2. For each sandwich, top one bread slice with one cheese slice, ¼ cup chicken, mushrooms, roasted peppers, another cheese slice and another bread slice. Brush outsides of sandwiches with remaining vinaigrette.

3. Preheat panini press, indoor grill or grill pan. Cook sandwiches until bread is golden brown and cheese is melted.

Tip A rotisserie chicken will yield just enough chopped chicken for this recipe.

Pita Bread

MAKES 8 PITA BREADS

3½ cups all-purpose flour

1 tablespoon salt

1 tablespoon sugar

1 package (¼ ounce) instant yeast (2¼ teaspoons)

1½ cups warm water (120°F)

2 tablespoons olive oil

1. Combine flour, salt, sugar and yeast in large bowl; whisk until well blended. Add 1½ cups water and oil; stir with wooden spoon until rough dough forms. If dough appears too dry, add additional 1 to 2 tablespoons water. Knead on lightly floured surface 5 to 7 minutes or until dough is smooth and elastic. Or knead with electric mixer using dough hook at low speed 5 minutes.

2. Shape dough into a ball. Place dough in large greased bowl; turn to grease top. Cover and let rise in warm place 1 hour or until doubled in size.

3. Preheat oven to 500°F. Turn out dough onto lightly floured surface; press into circle. Cut dough into eight wedges. Roll each wedge into a smooth ball; flatten slightly. Let rest 10 minutes.

4. Roll each ball into a circle about ¼ inch thick. Place on two ungreased baking sheets.

5. Bake 5 minutes or until pitas are puffed and set. Remove to wire rack to cool slightly.

Mediterranean Roasted Vegetable Wraps

MAKES 4 SERVINGS

1 head cauliflower, cut into 1-inch florets

4 tablespoons olive oil, divided

2 teaspoons ras el hanout, 7-spice blend, shawarma blend or za'atar

1 teaspoon salt, divided

1 zucchini, quartered lengthwise and cut into ¼-inch pieces

1 yellow squash, quartered lengthwise and cut into ¼-inch pieces

½ red onion, thinly sliced

¼ cup red pepper sauce (avjar)

4 large thin pita breads or lavash (10 inches)

1 cup (4 ounces) crumbled feta cheese

1 cup chickpeas

¼ cup diced tomatoes

¼ cup minced fresh parsley

¼ cup diced cucumber (optional)

2 teaspoons vegetable oil

1. Preheat oven to 400°F. Combine cauliflower, 2 tablespoons olive oil, ras el hanout and ½ teaspoon salt in large bowl; toss to coat. Spread on half of sheet pan. Combine zucchini, yellow squash, onion, remaining 2 tablespoons olive oil and ½ teaspoon salt in same bowl; toss to coat. Spread on other side of sheet pan. Roast 25 minutes or until vegetables are browned and tender, stirring once. Remove from oven; cool slightly.

2. Spread 1 tablespoon red pepper sauce on one pita. Top with one fourth of vegetables, feta, chickpeas, tomatoes, parsley and cucumber, if desired. Fold two sides over filling; roll up into burrito shape. Repeat with remaining ingredients.

3. Heat 1 teaspoon vegetable oil in large skillet over medium-high heat. Add two wraps, seam sides down; cook 1 minute or until browned. Turn and cook other side until browned. Repeat with remaining vegetable oil and wraps. Cut in half to serve.

Chicken and Roasted Tomato Panini

MAKES 4 SERVINGS

12 ounces plum tomatoes (about 2 large), cut into ⅛-inch slices

½ teaspoon salt, divided

¼ teaspoon black pepper, divided

2 tablespoons olive oil, divided

4 boneless skinless chicken breasts (about 6 ounces each)

3 tablespoons butter, softened

¼ teaspoon garlic powder

¼ cup mayonnaise

2 tablespoons pesto sauce

8 slices sourdough or rustic Italian bread

8 slices (about 1 ounce each) provolone cheese

½ cup baby spinach

1. Preheat oven to 400°F. Line baking sheet with parchment paper. Arrange tomato slices in single layer on prepared baking sheet. Sprinkle with ¼ teaspoon salt and ⅛ teaspoon pepper; drizzle with 1 tablespoon oil. Roast 25 minutes or until tomatoes are softened and begin to caramelize around edges.

2. Meanwhile, prepare chicken. If chicken breasts are thicker than ½ inch, pound to ½-inch thickness. Heat remaining 1 tablespoon oil in large skillet over medium-high heat. Season both sides of chicken with remaining ¼ teaspoon salt and ⅛ teaspoon pepper. Add to skillet; cook about 6 minutes per side or until golden brown and cooked through (165°F). Remove to plate; let stand 10 minutes before slicing. Cut diagonally into ½-inch slices.

3. Combine butter and garlic powder in small bowl; mix well. Combine mayonnaise and pesto in another small bowl; mix well.

4. Spread one side of each bread slice with garlic butter. For each sandwich, place one bread slice, buttered side down, on plate. Spread with generous 1 tablespoon pesto mayonnaise. Layer with one cheese slice, 4 to 5 roasted tomato slices, 4 to 6 spinach leaves, one sliced chicken breast, second cheese slice and 4 to 6 spinach leaves. Top with second bread slice, buttered side up.

5. Preheat panini press, indoor grill or grill pan. Cook sandwiches until bread is golden brown and cheese is melted.

Mediterranean Stuffed Pita

MAKES 6 SERVINGS

1¼ pounds chicken tenders, cut crosswise in half

½ teaspoon salt, divided

1 tablespoon olive oil

1 large tomato, diced

½ small cucumber, halved lengthwise, seeded and sliced

½ cup sweet onion slices (about 1 small)

2 tablespoons cider vinegar

1 tablespoon olive or canola oil

3 teaspoons minced fresh oregano *or* ½ teaspoon dried oregano

2 teaspoons minced fresh mint *or* ¼ teaspoon dried mint

6 (6-inch) whole wheat pita bread rounds, cut in half crosswise

12 lettuce leaves (optional)

1. Season chicken with ¼ teaspoon salt. Heat oil in large nonstick skillet over medium heat. Add chicken; cook and stir 7 to 10 minutes or until lightly browned and cooked through (165°F). Let stand 5 to 10 minutes to cool slightly.

2. Combine chicken, tomato, cucumber and onion in medium bowl. Add vinegar, oil, oregano, mint and remaining ¼ teaspoon salt; toss to coat.

3. Place one lettuce leaf in each pita half, if desired. Divide chicken mixture evenly among pita bread halves.

Greek Flat Breads

MAKES 16 FLAT BREADS

3 to 4 cups bread or all-purpose flour, divided

1 package (¼ ounce) active dry yeast (2¼ teaspoons)

2 tablespoons sugar

1 teaspoon salt

1 cup warm milk (120°F)

2 eggs, divided

2 tablespoons butter, softened

4 ounces crumbled feta cheese

½ cup chopped kalamata olives

3 cloves garlic, minced

1 tablespoon olive oil

2 tablespoons water

1. Combine 3 cups flour, yeast, sugar and salt in large bowl of electric mixer; attach dough hook to mixer. Add milk, 1 egg and butter; knead on low speed 5 to 7 minutes or until dough is smooth and elastic and cleans side of bowl, adding additional flour by tablespoons if needed. Shape dough into a ball. Place in large lightly greased bowl; turn to grease top. Cover and let rise in warm place about 1 hour or until doubled in size.

2. Grease baking sheet or line with parchment paper. Turn out dough onto lightly oiled surface; divide into 16 equal pieces. Shape each piece into a ball. Cover with towel; let rest 5 minutes.

3. Combine feta, olives, garlic and oil in medium bowl. Beat remaining egg and water in small bowl.

4. Flatten each ball of dough to ½-inch thickness. Place 2 inches apart on prepared baking sheet. Brush dough with beaten egg; sprinkle evenly with feta mixture, pressing into dough slightly. Cover and let rise 45 minutes. Preheat oven to 400°F.

5. Bake 15 minutes or until breads are lightly browned. Immediately remove to wire rack to cool.

Roasted Eggplant Panini

MAKES 4 SANDWICHES

1 medium eggplant (about 1¼ pounds)

4 tablespoons olive oil

Salt and black pepper

1 cup (4 ounces) shredded mozzarella cheese

1 tablespoon lemon juice

1 tablespoon chopped fresh basil

⅛ teaspoon salt

8 slices whole grain Italian bread

1. Preheat oven to 400°F. Line baking sheet with parchment paper. Slice eggplant in half lengthwise; brush both sides with 1 tablespoon oil and season lightly with salt and pepper. Place on prepared baking sheet. Roast 45 minutes. Let stand 15 minutes or until cool enough to handle.

2. Meanwhile, combine cheese, lemon juice, basil and salt in small bowl; mix well.

3. Cut each eggplant piece in half. Remove pulp; discard skin. Place one fourth of eggplant on each of four bread slices, pressing gently into bread. Top evenly with cheese mixture and remaining bread slices. Brush sandwiches with remaining 3 tablespoons oil.

4. Heat large nonstick grill pan or skillet over medium heat. Cook sandwiches 3 to 4 minutes per side or until cheese is melted and bread is toasted, pressing down with spatula. (Cover pan during last minute of cooking to melt cheese, if desired.) Serve immediately.

Pesto Veggie Sandwich

MAKES 4 SERVINGS

1 pound cremini mushrooms, stemmed and thinly sliced (⅛ inch slices)

2 tablespoons olive oil, divided

¾ teaspoon salt, divided

¼ teaspoon black pepper

1 medium zucchini, diced (¼ inch pieces, about 2 cups)

3 tablespoons butter, softened

8 slices artisan whole grain bread

¼ cup prepared pesto

¼ cup mayonnaise

2 cups packed baby spinach

4 slices (1 ounce each) mozzarella cheese

1. Preheat oven to 350°F. Combine mushrooms, 1 tablespoon oil, ½ teaspoon salt and pepper in medium bowl; toss to coat. Spread in single layer on large rimmed baking sheet. Roast 20 minutes or until mushrooms are dark brown and dry, stirring after 10 minutes. Cool on baking sheet.

2. Meanwhile, heat remaining 1 tablespoon oil in large skillet over medium heat. Add zucchini and remaining ¼ teaspoon salt; cook and stir 5 minutes or until zucchini is tender and lightly browned. Remove to medium bowl; wipe out skillet with paper towels.

3. Spread butter on one side of each bread slice. Turn over slices. Spread pesto on four bread slices; spread mayonnaise on remaining four slices. Top pesto-covered slices evenly with mushrooms; layer with spinach, zucchini and cheese. Top with remaining bread slices, mayonnaise side down.

4. Heat same skillet over medium heat. Add sandwiches; cover and cook 2 minutes per side or until bread is toasted, spinach is slightly wilted and cheese is beginning to melt. Serve immediately.

Tomato and Cheese Focaccia

MAKES 8 SERVINGS

1 package (¼ ounce) active dry yeast (2¼ teaspoons)

¾ cup warm water (105° to 115°F)

2 cups all-purpose flour

½ teaspoon salt

4½ tablespoons olive oil, divided

1 teaspoon Italian seasoning

8 oil-packed sun-dried tomatoes, well drained

½ cup (2 ounces) shredded provolone cheese

¼ cup grated Parmesan cheese

1. Dissolve yeast in warm water in small bowl; let stand 5 minutes or until bubbly. Combine flour and salt in food processor. Add yeast mixture and 3 tablespoons oil; pulse until dough forms a ball. Process 1 minute.

2. Turn out dough onto lightly floured surface. Knead about 2 minutes or until dough is smooth and elastic. Shape into a ball. Place dough in greased bowl; turn to grease top. Cover and let rise in warm place about 30 minutes or until doubled in size.

3. Brush 10-inch round cake pan, deep-dish pizza pan or springform pan with ½ tablespoon oil. Punch down dough; let rest 5 minutes.

4. Press dough into prepared pan. Brush with remaining 1 tablespoon oil; sprinkle with Italian seasoning. Press sun-dried tomatoes into top of dough; sprinkle with provolone and Parmesan. Cover and let rise in warm place 15 minutes. Preheat oven to 425°F.

5. Bake 20 to 25 minutes or until golden brown. Remove to wire rack; cool slightly. Cut into wedges.

Note To mix dough by hand, combine flour and salt in large bowl. Stir in yeast mixture and 3 tablespoons oil until a ball forms. Turn out onto lightly floured surface and knead about 10 minutes or until smooth and elastic. Proceed as directed.

Pasta & Grains

Pasta Primavera

MAKES 4 SERVINGS

8 ounces uncooked linguine

1 tablespoon olive oil

2 green onions, sliced diagonally

1 clove garlic, minced

1 cup sliced mushrooms

1 cup broccoli florets

2½ cups fresh snow peas

4 asparagus spears, cut into 2-inch pieces

1 red bell pepper, cut into thin strips

½ teaspoon dried tarragon

½ teaspoon salt

½ teaspoon black pepper

½ cup Greek yogurt or crème fraîche

⅓ cup grated Parmesan cheese

1. Cook pasta in large saucepan of salted boiling water according to package directions for al dente. Drain, reserving ½ cup cooking water. Place pasta in serving bowl; keep warm.

2. Meanwhile, heat oil in large nonstick skillet over medium heat. Add green onions and garlic; cook and stir 2 to 3 minutes or until softened. Add mushrooms and broccoli; cover and cook 3 minutes or until mushrooms are tender. Add snow peas, asparagus, bell pepper, tarragon, salt and black pepper; cook and stir until vegetables are crisp-tender. Stir in yogurt and cheese.

3. Pour vegetables over pasta; mix well, adding reserved pasta water by tablespoons to loosen sauce.

Eggplant Parmesan

MAKES 4 SERVINGS

4 tablespoons olive oil, divided

2 cloves garlic, minced

1 can (28 ounces) whole tomatoes, undrained

½ cup water

1¼ teaspoons salt, divided

¼ teaspoon dried oregano

Pinch red pepper flakes

1 package (16 ounces) uncooked spaghetti

Black pepper

1 medium eggplant (about 1 pound)

⅓ cup all-purpose flour

⅔ cup milk

1 egg

1 cup Italian-seasoned dry bread crumbs

5 tablespoons vegetable oil, divided

1 cup (4 ounces) shredded mozzarella cheese

Chopped fresh parsley (optional)

1. Heat 2 tablespoons olive oil in medium saucepan over medium heat. Add garlic; cook and stir 1 minute. Crush tomatoes with hands over saucepan or chop and add to saucepan with juice. Stir in water, 1 teaspoon salt, oregano and red pepper flakes; bring to a simmer. Reduce heat to medium-low; cook 45 minutes, stirring occasionally.

2. Cook pasta in large saucepan of salted boiling water according to package directions for al dente. Drain and return to saucepan; stir in remaining 2 tablespoons olive oil and season with black pepper. Keep warm.

3. Meanwhile, cut eggplant crosswise into ¼-inch slices. Combine flour, remaining ¼ teaspoon salt and black pepper in shallow dish. Beat milk and egg in another shallow dish. Place bread crumbs in third shallow dish. Coat both sides of eggplant slices with flour mixture, shaking off excess. Dip in egg mixture, letting excess drip back into dish. Roll in bread crumbs to coat.

4. Heat 3 tablespoons vegetable oil in large skillet over medium-high heat. Working in batches, add eggplant slices to skillet in single layer; cook 3 to 4 minutes per side or until golden brown, adding additional vegetable oil as needed. Remove to paper towel-lined plate; cover loosely with foil to keep warm.

5. Preheat broiler. Spray 13×9-inch baking dish with nonstick cooking spray. Arrange eggplant slices overlapping in baking dish; top with half of warm marinara sauce. Sprinkle with cheese. Broil 2 to 3 minutes or just until cheese is melted and beginning to brown. Serve eggplant and remaining sauce with pasta. Garnish with parsley.

Pesto Cavatappi

MAKES 4 TO 6 SERVINGS

Pesto

2 cups packed fresh basil leaves*

1 cup walnuts, toasted**

½ cup shredded Parmesan cheese, plus additional for garnish

4 cloves garlic

1 teaspoon salt

¼ teaspoon black pepper

¾ cup olive oil

Or substitute 1 cup packed fresh parsley leaves for half of basil.

**To toast walnuts, cook in medium skillet over medium heat 4 to 5 minutes or lightly browned, stirring frequently.*

Pasta

1 package (16 ounces) uncooked cavatappi pasta

1 tablespoon olive oil

2 plum tomatoes, diced (1½ cups)

1 package (8 ounces) sliced mushrooms

¼ cup dry white wine

¼ cup vegetable broth

¼ cup whipping cream

1. For pesto, combine basil, walnuts, ½ cup cheese, garlic, salt and pepper in food processor; pulse until coarsely chopped. With motor running, add ¾ cup oil in thin, steady stream; process until well blended. Measure 1 cup pesto for pasta; reserve remaining pesto for another use.

2. Cook pasta in large saucepan of salted boiling water according to package directions until al dente. Drain and return to saucepan; keep warm.

3. Meanwhile, heat 1 tablespoon oil in large skillet over medium-high heat. Add tomatoes and mushrooms; cook about 7 minutes or until most of liquid has evaporated, stirring occasionally. Add wine, broth and cream; bring to a boil. Reduce heat to low; cook and stir about 4 minutes or until sauce has thickened slightly. Stir in 1 cup pesto; cook just until heated through.

4. Pour sauce over pasta; stir gently to coat. Divide pasta among serving bowls; garnish with additional cheese.

Pasta e Ceci

MAKES 4 SERVINGS

4 tablespoons olive oil, divided

1 onion, chopped

1 carrot, chopped

1 clove garlic, minced

1 sprig fresh rosemary

1 teaspoon salt

1 can (28 ounces) whole tomatoes, drained and crushed (see Tip)

2 cups vegetable broth

1 can (about 15 ounces) chickpeas, undrained

1 bay leaf

⅛ teaspoon red pepper flakes

1 cup uncooked orecchiette pasta

Salt and black pepper (optional)

Chopped fresh parsley or basil (optional)

1. Heat 3 tablespoons oil in large saucepan over medium-high heat. Add onion and carrot; cook 10 minutes or until vegetables are soft, stirring occasionally.

2. Add garlic, rosemary and 1 teaspoon salt; cook and stir 1 minute. Stir in tomatoes, broth, chickpeas with liquid, bay leaf and red pepper flakes. Remove 1 cup mixture to food processor or blender; process until smooth. Stir back into saucepan; bring to a boil.

3. Stir in pasta. Reduce heat to medium; cook 12 to 15 minutes or until pasta is tender and mixture is creamy. Remove and discard bay leaf and rosemary sprig. Taste and season with additional salt and black pepper, if desired. Divide evenly among bowls; garnish with parsley and drizzle with remaining 1 tablespoon oil.

Tip To crush the tomatoes, take them out of the can one at a time and crush them between your fingers over the pot, or coarsely chop them with a knife.

Kale, Gorgonzola and Noodles

MAKES 6 SERVINGS

1 large bunch kale, stemmed and coarsely chopped (about 8 cups)

2 tablespoons butter

¼ cup chopped green onions

1 small clove garlic, smashed

2 tablespoons all-purpose flour

2¼ cups half-and-half

4 ounces gorgonzola cheese, crumbled

4 ounces fontina cheese, cut into small chunks

½ teaspoon salt

¼ teaspoon pepper

¼ teaspoon ground nutmeg

6 ounces uncooked egg noodles or fettuccine, cooked

¼ cup coarse dry bread crumbs

1. Preheat oven to 350°F. Spray 9-inch square baking dish with nonstick cooking spray.

2. Place kale in large saucepan with 1 inch of water. Cover; bring to a simmer. Cook 15 minutes or until kale is tender. Drain well, pressing out excess liquid, and set aside.

3. Melt butter in large saucepan or deep skillet over medium-low heat. Add green onions and garlic; cook and stir over low heat 5 minutes. Discard garlic. Whisk in flour until paste forms. Gradually whisk in half-and-half; cook until mixture is thickened, whisking frequently. Gradually stir in cheeses until melted. Stir in salt, pepper and nutmeg. Stir in noodles and kale; mix well.

4. Spoon into prepared baking dish. Sprinkle with bread crumbs. Bake 30 minutes or until bubbly and top is browned.

Pesto Pasta with Scallops

MAKES 4 SERVINGS

- 8 ounces uncooked whole wheat rotini
- 3 tablespoons olive oil, divided
- 12 ounces asparagus (about 20 spears), cut into 2-inch-pieces
- 8 ounces cherry tomatoes, halved (about 2 cups)
- ½ teaspoon salt, divided
- ½ teaspoon black pepper, divided
- 12 ounces large sea scallops
- 1 tablespoon lemon juice
- 1 clove garlic, minced
- 6 tablespoons prepared pesto
- 3 tablespoons Greek yogurt
- Pinch red pepper flakes (optional)

1. Cook pasta in large saucepan of salted boiling water according to package directions for al dente. Drain and return to saucepan; keep warm.

2. Meanwhile, heat 1 tablespoon oil in medium skillet over medium heat. Add asparagus; cook 5 minutes, stirring occasionally. Add tomatoes, ¼ teaspoon salt and ¼ teaspoon black pepper; cover and cook over low heat about 5 minutes, stirring occasionally. Add to pasta; keep warm.

3. Combine scallops, 1 tablespoon oil, lemon juice, garlic and remaining ¼ teaspoon black pepper in large bowl; toss to coat.

4. Heat remaining 1 tablespoon oil in same skillet over medium-high heat. Add scallops and remaining ¼ teaspoon salt; cook about 3 minutes per side or until scallops are opaque.

5. Combine pesto, yogurt and red pepper flakes, if desired, in small bowl until blended. Add to pasta mixture; stir gently to coat. Arrange scallops over pasta.

Grilled Veggies and Couscous

MAKES 6 SERVINGS

⅓ cup pine nuts

1½ cups vegetable broth or water

2 tablespoons olive oil, divided

½ teaspoon salt

1 cup uncooked couscous

1 medium zucchini, cut lengthwise into ½-inch slices

1 red bell pepper, cut in half

½ small red onion, sliced

¼ cup crumbled feta or basil-tomato flavored feta cheese

1 clove garlic, minced

Salt and black pepper

½ teaspoon lemon-pepper seasoning

1. Toast pine nuts in small nonstick skillet over medium heat 5 minutes or just until light brown and fragrant, stirring frequently. Cool completely on plate.

2. Combine broth, 1 tablespoon oil and ½ teaspoon salt in small saucepan; bring to a boil over medium-high heat. Stir in couscous. Remove from heat; cover and set aside.

3. Prepare grill for direct cooking. Brush vegetables with remaining 1 tablespoon oil. Place vegetables on grid over medium-high heat. Grill zucchini and onion 3 to 5 minutes until tender. Grill bell pepper 7 to 10 minutes or until skin is blackened. Place pepper in small plastic bag; seal and set aside 3 to 5 minutes. Remove from bag; peel off blackened skin. Chop vegetables.

4. Spoon couscous into serving bowl; fluff with fork. Add vegetables, pine nuts, cheese, garlic, salt and black pepper; mix well. Sprinkle with lemon-pepper seasoning.

Mediterranean Orzo and Vegetable Pilaf

MAKES 6 SERVINGS

¾ cup uncooked orzo pasta

1 tablespoon olive oil

1 small onion, diced

2 cloves garlic, minced

1 small zucchini, diced

½ cup vegetable broth or water

1 can (about 14 ounces) artichoke hearts, drained and quartered

1 medium tomato, chopped

½ teaspoon dried oregano

½ teaspoon salt

¼ teaspoon black pepper

½ cup (2 ounces) crumbled feta cheese

Sliced black olives (optional)

1. Cook orzo in medium saucepan of salted boiling water according to package directions for al dente. Drain and return to saucepan.

2. Heat oil in large nonstick skillet over medium heat over medium-high heat. Add onion; cook and stir 5 minutes or until translucent. Add garlic; cook and stir 1 minute. Reduce heat to low. Stir in zucchini and broth; cook 5 minutes or until zucchini is crisp-tender.

3. Add cooked orzo, artichokes, tomato, oregano, salt and pepper; cook and stir 1 minute or until heated through. Top with cheese and olives, if desired.

Fettuccine with Vegetable Marinara Sauce

MAKES 4 TO 6 SERVINGS

2 tablespoons olive oil

1 yellow onion, finely chopped

1 carrot, finely chopped

1 stalk celery, finely chopped

2 cloves garlic, finely chopped

1 can (28 ounces) whole tomatoes, undrained

½ cup water

⅓ cup packed chopped fresh basil leaves

Salt and black pepper

1 package (about 9 ounces) fresh fettuccine *or* 8 ounces uncooked dried fettuccine

2 tablespoons butter, thinly sliced

Shredded Parmesan cheese

1. Heat oil in large saucepan over medium heat. Add onion, carrot, celery and garlic; cook and stir about 5 minutes or until onion is golden and tender, stirring occasionally.

2. Drain tomatoes, reserving juice. Coarsely crush tomatoes with hands or coarsely chop. Add tomatoes, reserved juice and water to saucepan; bring to a boil over high heat. Reduce heat to medium-low; simmer about 45 minutes or until slightly thickened and reduced, stirring frequently. Stir in basil during last 5 minutes of cooking. Season to taste with salt and pepper.

3. Cook pasta in large saucepan of salted boiling water according to package directions until barely tender. Drain and return to saucepan. Add butter; stir gently until pasta is coated and butter is melted. Serve sauce over pasta; top with Parmesan.

Lentils with Pasta

MAKES 6 TO 8 SERVINGS

1 cup dried lentils

1 cup dried split peas

1 tablespoon olive oil

1 onion, chopped

2 tablespoons tomato paste

2 cloves garlic, minced

1 teaspoon salt

¼ teaspoon black pepper

1 can (about 14 ounces) diced tomatoes

3 cups water

12 ounces uncooked short pasta (elbow macaroni, small shells, ditalini or similar)

Shredded Romano or Parmesan cheese (optional)

1. Place lentils and split peas in medium bowl; cover with water. Let stand at least 10 minutes.

2. Heat oil in large saucepan or Dutch oven over medium-high heat. Add onion; cook and stir 5 minutes or until onion is lightly browned. Add tomato paste, garlic, salt and pepper; cook and stir 1 minute. Add tomatoes and 3 cups water; bring to a boil.

3. Drain lentils and split peas and add to saucepan. Reduce heat to medium-low; cover and simmer about 40 minutes or until lentils and split peas are tender.

4. Meanwhile, cook pasta in large saucepan of boiling salted water according to package directions for al dente. Drain and add to lentil mixture; mix well. Serve with cheese, if desired.

Fresh Seafood and Linguine Salad

MAKES 6 SERVINGS

1½ pounds small squid

4 pounds mussels, cleaned*

1½ to 3 dozen clams*

8 ounces uncooked linguine

½ cup plus 3 tablespoons olive oil, divided

¼ cup lemon juice

2 cloves garlic, minced

½ teaspoon salt

¼ teaspoon black pepper

Red onion slivers (optional)

Finely chopped Italian parsley (optional)

Discard any opened clams or mussels.

1. Clean squid. Cut bodies crosswise into ¼-inch rings; finely chop tentacles and fins. Pat pieces dry with paper towels.

2. To steam clams and mussels, bring 1 cup water to a boil in large saucepan or Dutch oven over high heat. Add clams and mussels. Reduce heat to low; cover and steam 5 to 7 minutes or until clams and mussels are opened. Remove to large bowl with slotted spoon. Discard any clams or mussels that remain closed.

3. Meanwhile, cook pasta in large saucepan of salted boiling water according to package directions for al dente. Drain and return to saucepan; toss with 1 tablespoon oil.

4. Heat 2 tablespoons oil in large saucepan over medium heat. Add squid; cook and stir 2 minutes or until opaque. Add squid to bowl with clams and mussels. Stir in linguine.

5. Whisk remaining ½ cup olive oil, lemon juice, garlic, salt and pepper in small bowl until blended. Pour over pasta mixture; toss gently to coat. Cover and refrigerate at least 3 hours before serving. Season with additional lemon juice, salt and pepper. Garnish with onion and parsley.

Pastitsio

MAKES 6 SERVINGS

8 ounces uncooked ziti pasta or elbow macaroni

1 pound ground lamb or beef

½ cup chopped onion

1 clove garlic, minced

1 can (8 ounces) tomato sauce

½ teaspoon dried oregano

½ teaspoon salt

½ teaspoon black pepper

¼ teaspoon ground cinnamon

2 tablespoons butter

2 tablespoons all-purpose flour

1½ cups milk

1 egg

1 cup grated Parmesan cheese, divided

1. Preheat oven to 350°F. Spray 9-inch baking dish with nonstick cooking spray.

2. Cook pasta in large saucepan of salted boiling water according to package directions for al dente. Drain and return to saucepan; keep warm.

3. Brown lamb in large nonstick skillet over medium-high heat 6 to 8 minutes, stirring to break up meat. Drain all but 1 tablespoon fat. Add onion; cook and stir 2 minutes or until translucent. Add garlic; cook and stir 30 seconds. Stir in tomato sauce, oregano, salt, pepper and cinnamon. Reduce heat to low; simmer 10 minutes.

4. Spread half of pasta in prepared dish. Top with lamb mixture, then remaining pasta.

5. For sauce, melt butter in medium saucepan over medium-low heat. Whisk in flour until smooth; cook 1 minute, whisking constantly. Whisk in milk; cook 6 minutes or until thickened, whisking frequently. Beat egg in small bowl; stir in some of sauce. Return egg mixture to saucepan; cook 2 minutes, whisking frequently. Remove from heat; stir in ¾ cup cheese until smooth.

6. Pour sauce over top. Sprinkle with remaining ¼ cup cheese. Bake 30 minutes or until heated through and golden brown.

Spinach Stuffed Manicotti

MAKES 4 SERVINGS

8 uncooked manicotti pasta shells

2 teaspoons olive oil

1 teaspoon minced garlic

1 teaspoon dried rosemary

1 teaspoon dried sage

1 teaspoon dried oregano

1 teaspoon dried thyme

1½ cups chopped fresh tomatoes *or* 1 can (about 14 ounces) diced tomatoes

1 package (10 ounces) frozen spinach, thawed and squeezed dry

½ cup ricotta cheese

½ cup fresh whole wheat bread crumbs

Salt and black pepper

1 egg, lightly beaten

1. Preheat oven to 350°F. Cook pasta according to package directions; drain and rinse under cold water until cool enough to handle.

2. Heat oil in medium saucepan over medium heat. Add garlic, rosemary, sage, oregano and thyme; cook and stir about 1 minute. Stir in tomatoes. Reduce heat to low; simmer 10 minutes, stirring occasionally.

3. Combine spinach, cheese and bread crumbs in medium bowl; mix well. Season to taste with salt and pepper. Stir in egg. Fill manicotti shells with spinach mixture.

4. Pour one third of tomato sauce into 13×9-inch baking dish. Arrange manicotti in dish; pour remaining tomato sauce over manicotti. Cover with foil.

5. Bake 30 minutes or until hot and bubbly.

Vegetable Penne Italiano

MAKES 4 SERVINGS

1 tablespoon olive oil

1 red bell pepper, cut into ½-inch pieces

1 green bell pepper, cut into ½-inch pieces

1 medium sweet onion, halved and thinly sliced

3 cloves garlic, minced

2 tablespoons tomato paste

2 teaspoons salt

1 teaspoon sugar

1 teaspoon Italian seasoning

¼ teaspoon black pepper

1 can (28 ounces) whole tomatoes, undrained, chopped

8 ounces uncooked penne pasta

Grated Parmesan cheese

Chopped fresh basil

1. Heat oil in large skillet over medium-high heat. Add bell peppers, onion and garlic; cook and stir 8 minutes or until vegetables are crisp-tender.

2. Add tomato paste, salt, sugar, Italian seasoning and black pepper; cook and stir 1 minute. Stir in tomatoes with juice. Reduce heat to medium-low; cook 15 minutes or until vegetables are tender and sauce is thickened.

3. Meanwhile, cook pasta in large saucepan of salted boiling water according to package directions for al dente. Drain and return to saucepan. Pour sauce over pasta; stir gently to coat. Serve with cheese and basil.

Spaghetti Mediterranean

MAKES 4 SERVINGS

1½ pounds fresh tomatoes (about 4 large)

8 ounces uncooked spaghetti

¼ cup olive oil

2 cloves garlic, minced

½ cup chopped fresh parsley

12 pitted green olives, sliced

4 to 6 flat anchovy fillets, chopped

1 tablespoon drained capers

2 teaspoons chopped fresh basil *or* ½ teaspoon dried basil

½ teaspoon salt

½ teaspoon dried oregano

¼ teaspoon red pepper flakes

1. Bring large saucepan of water to a boil. Add tomatoes; cook 1 minute to loosen skins. Immediately drain tomatoes and rinse under cold water. Peel, seed and coarsely chop tomatoes.

2. Cook pasta in large saucepan of salted boiling water according to package directions for al dente. Drain and return to saucepan; keep warm.

3. Meanwhile, heat oil in large skillet over medium-high heat. Add garlic; cook about 30 seconds or just until garlic begins to turn golden. Stir in tomatoes, parsley, olives, anchovies, capers, basil, salt, oregano and red pepper flakes; cook and stir 10 minutes until most of liquid has evaporated and sauce is slightly thickened.

4. Pour sauce over spaghetti; toss gently to coat. Serve immediately.

Meats & Fish

Forty-Clove Chicken

MAKES 4 TO 6 SERVINGS

1 cut-up whole chicken (about 3 pounds)

Salt and black pepper

¼ cup olive oil

40 cloves garlic (about 2 heads), peeled

4 stalks celery, thickly sliced

½ cup dry white wine

¼ cup dry vermouth

Grated peel and juice of 1 lemon

2 tablespoons finely chopped fresh parsley

2 teaspoons dried basil

1 teaspoon dried oregano

Pinch red pepper flakes

1. Preheat oven to 375°F.

2. Season chicken all over with salt and pepper. Heat oil in Dutch oven over medium-high heat. Add chicken; cook until browned on all sides.

3. Combine garlic, celery, wine, vermouth, lemon peel and juice, parsley, basil, oregano and red pepper flakes in medium bowl; pour over chicken.

4. Cover and bake 40 minutes. Remove cover; bake 15 minutes or until chicken is cooked through (165°F). Season with additional salt and pepper, if desired.

Chicken Saltimbocca

MAKES 4 SERVINGS

4 boneless skinless chicken breasts (about 6 ounces each)*

¼ teaspoon salt

2 tablespoons chopped fresh sage

4 thin slices prosciutto

1 to 2 tablespoons all-purpose flour

2 tablespoons olive oil

⅓ cup dry white wine

1 can (about 14 ounces) quartered artichoke hearts, drained

¼ cup whipping cream

2 tablespoons butter, cut into pieces

2 tablespoons lemon juice

2 tablespoons capers, rinsed and drained

Chopped fresh parsley (optional)

Or use two large chicken breasts (12 to 14 ounces each and 1 inch thick). Cut each in half horizontally with a sharp knife so each piece is about ½ inch thick.

1. Pound chicken breasts to even thickness (about ½ inch thick) between two sheets of waxed paper or plastic wrap with meat mallet or rolling pin. Season both sides of chicken with salt. Sprinkle one side of each chicken breast with sage; top with prosciutto slice. Pound chicken again so prosciutto adheres to chicken and flattens slightly. (Chicken should be between ¼ and ½ inch thick.) Dust both sides lightly with flour.

2. Heat oil in large skillet over medium-high heat. Add chicken, prosciutto sides down; cook about 5 minutes per side or until browned and cooked through (165°F). Remove chicken to platter; tent with foil to keep warm. Drain excess fat from skillet if necessary.

3. Add wine to skillet; cook 2 minutes, scraping up browned bits from bottom of skillet. Add artichokes, cream, butter and lemon juice; cook about 4 minutes or until sauce thickens and artichokes are heated through.

4. Pour sauce over chicken; sprinkle with capers and parsley, if desired.

Chicken Scarpiello

MAKES 6 SERVINGS

3 tablespoons olive oil, divided

1 pound spicy Italian sausage, cut into 1-inch pieces

1 whole chicken (about 3 pounds), cut into 10 pieces*

1 teaspoon salt, divided

1 large onion, chopped

2 red, yellow or orange bell peppers, cut into ¼-inch strips

3 cloves garlic, minced

½ cup dry white wine

½ cup chicken broth

½ cup coarsely chopped seeded hot cherry peppers

½ cup liquid from cherry pepper jar

1 teaspoon dried oregano

¼ cup chopped fresh parsley

Or, purchase 2 bone-in chicken leg quarters and 2 chicken breasts; separate drumsticks and thighs and cut breasts in half.

1. Heat 1 tablespoon oil in large skillet over medium-high heat. Add sausage; cook about 10 minutes or until well browned on all sides, stirring occasionally. Remove to plate.

2. Heat 1 tablespoon oil in same skillet. Sprinkle chicken with ½ teaspoon salt; arrange skin side down in single layer in skillet (cook in batches, if necessary). Cook about 6 minutes per side or until browned. Remove to plate. Drain fat from skillet.

3. Heat remaining 1 tablespoon oil in skillet. Add onion and ½ teaspoon salt; cook and stir 2 minutes or until softened, scraping up browned bits from bottom of skillet. Add bell peppers and garlic; cook and stir 5 minutes. Stir in wine; cook until liquid is reduced by half. Stir in broth, cherry peppers, cherry pepper liquid and oregano. Season with additional salt and black pepper; bring to a simmer.

4. Return sausage and chicken along with any accumulated juices to skillet. Partially cover and cook 10 minutes. Uncover and cook 15 minutes or until chicken is cooked through (165°F). Sprinkle with parsley.

Mediterranean Chicken Kabobs

MAKES 8 SERVINGS

2 pounds boneless skinless chicken breasts or chicken tenders, cut into 1-inch pieces

1 each red, yellow and green bell pepper, cut into 1-inch pieces

2 medium onions, each cut into thin wedges

1 cup chicken broth

⅔ cup balsamic vinegar

3 tablespoons olive oil

2 tablespoons dried mint

1 tablespoon dried basil

1 tablespoon dried oregano

2 teaspoons salt

1. Alternately thread chicken, bell peppers and onions onto 16 bamboo skewers; place in large glass baking dish.

2. Combine broth, vinegar, oil, mint, basil, oregano and salt in small bowl; pour over kabobs. Cover; marinate in refrigerator 2 hours, turning occasionally. Remove kabobs from marinade; discard marinade.

3. Spray grid with nonstick cooking spray; prepare grill for direct cooking over medium-high heat. Grill kabobs, covered, 10 to 15 minutes or until the chicken is cooked through, turning once.

Swordfish Pomodoro

MAKES 6 SERVINGS

1½ pounds swordfish steaks (¾ inch thick)

Salt and black pepper

2 tablespoons all-purpose flour

3 tablespoons olive oil, divided

1 medium onion, halved and cut into thin slices

1 clove garlic, minced

1½ cups chopped seeded tomatoes

⅓ cup drained mild giardiniera

2 tablespoons dry white wine (optional)

1 tablespoon chopped fresh oregano *or* 1 teaspoon dried oregano

1. Season fish with salt and pepper. Place flour in shallow dish; dredge fish in flour, shaking off excess.

2. Heat 1 tablespoon oil in medium skillet over medium heat. Add onion; cook and stir 4 minutes or until translucent. Add garlic; cook and stir 30 seconds. Add tomatoes; cook 3 minutes, stirring occasionally. Stir in giardiniera, wine, if desired, and oregano; cook 3 minutes or until most liquid is evaporated.

3. Heat remaining 2 tablespoons oil in large nonstick skillet over medium-high heat. Add fish; cook 4 minutes on each side or until fish begins to flake when tested with fork. Serve tomato mixture over fish.

Midweek Moussaka

MAKES 4 SERVINGS

1 eggplant (about 1 pound), cut into ¼-inch slices

2 tablespoons olive oil

1 pound ground beef

1 can (about 14 ounces) stewed tomatoes, drained

¼ cup red wine

2 tablespoons tomato paste

2 teaspoons sugar

¾ teaspoon salt

½ teaspoon dried oregano

¼ teaspoon ground cinnamon

¼ teaspoon black pepper

⅛ teaspoon ground allspice

4 ounces cream cheese

¼ cup milk

¼ cup grated Parmesan cheese

Additional ground cinnamon (optional)

1. Preheat broiler. Spray 8-inch square baking dish with nonstick cooking spray.

2. Line baking sheet with foil. Arrange eggplant slices on foil, overlapping slightly if necessary. Brush with oil; broil 5 to 6 inches from heat 4 minutes on each side. *Reduce oven temperature to 350°F.*

3. Meanwhile, brown beef in large nonstick skillet over medium-high heat 6 to 8 minutes, stirring to break up meat. Drain fat. Add tomatoes, wine, tomato paste, sugar, salt, oregano, cinnamon, pepper and allspice. Bring to a boil, breaking up large pieces of tomato with spoon. Reduce heat to medium-low; cover and simmer 10 minutes.

4. Place cream cheese and milk in small microwavable bowl. Cover and microwave on HIGH 1 minute.* Stir with fork until smooth.

5. Arrange half of eggplant slices in prepared baking dish. Spoon half of meat sauce over eggplant; sprinkle with half of Parmesan cheese. Repeat layers. Spoon cream cheese mixture evenly over top. Bake 20 minutes or until top begins to crack slightly. Sprinkle lightly with additional cinnamon, if desired. Let stand 10 minutes before serving.

Or place in small saucepan over medium heat and stir until cream cheese has melted.

Tuscan Chicken with Polenta

MAKES 8 SERVINGS

1 teaspoon salt, divided

½ teaspoon garlic powder

½ teaspoon Italian seasoning

¼ teaspoon black pepper

4 boneless skinless chicken breasts
(about 2 pounds)

4 tablespoons olive oil, divided

½ cup chopped onion

2 cloves garlic, minced

8 plum tomatoes, coarsely chopped

1 can (8 ounces) tomato sauce

2 teaspoons dried basil

2 teaspoons dried oregano

2 teaspoons dried rosemary

½ teaspoon black pepper

1 tube (18 ounces) prepared polenta

1. Preheat oven to 350°F. Combine ½ teaspoon salt, garlic powder, Italian seasoning and pepper in small bowl; rub all over chicken. Arrange chicken in single layer in 13×9-inch baking pan. Bake about 30 minutes or until chicken is cooked through (165°F).

2. Meanwhile for sauce, heat 2 tablespoons oil medium saucepan over medium heat. Add onion and garlic; cook and stir about 5 minutes or until tender. Stir in tomatoes, tomato sauce, basil, oregano, rosemary, remaining ½ teaspoon salt and pepper; bring to a boil. Reduce heat to medium-low; simmer, uncovered, about 6 minutes or until desired consistency is reached, stirring occasionally.

3. Cut polenta crosswise into 16 slices; cut slices into triangles, if desired. Heat remaining 2 tablespoons oil in large nonstick skillet over medium heat. Add polenta; cook about 4 minutes per side or until lightly browned. Serve with chicken and sauce.

Lemon Rosemary Shrimp and Vegetable Souvlaki

MAKES 4 KABOBS

8 ounces large raw shrimp, peeled and deveined (with tails on)

1 medium zucchini, halved lengthwise and cut into ½-inch slices

½ medium red bell pepper, cut into 1-inch squares

8 green onions, trimmed and cut into 2-inch pieces

2 tablespoons olive oil

2 tablespoons lemon juice

2 teaspoons grated lemon peel

2 cloves garlic, minced

½ teaspoon salt

½ teaspoon fresh rosemary

⅛ teaspoon red pepper flakes

1. Prepare grill for direct cooking. Spray grid or grill pan with nonstick cooking spray.

2. Spray four 12-inch bamboo or metal skewers with cooking spray. (If using bamboo skewers, soak in water 20 to 30 minutes before using to prevent burning.) Alternately thread shrimp, zucchini, bell pepper and green onions onto skewers. Spray with cooking spray.

3. For dressing, combine oil, lemon juice, lemon peel, garlic, salt, rosemary and red pepper flakes in small bowl; mix well.

4. Grill skewers over high heat 2 minutes per side. Remove to large serving platter; drizzle with dressing.

Greek Braised Cinnamon Chicken

MAKES 4 SERVINGS

4 chicken leg quarters (drumstick and thigh, 8 to 10 ounces each)

1¾ teaspoons salt, divided

¾ teaspoon black pepper, divided

¼ plus ⅛ teaspoon ground cinnamon, divided

2 tablespoons olive oil

2 medium onions, chopped

3 cloves garlic, minced

1 can (28 ounces) whole tomatoes, undrained, coarsely chopped or crushed with hands

½ cup chicken broth

1 cinnamon stick

Chopped fresh parsley

Grated Kasseri* or Romano cheese (optional)

Kasseri is a semi-hard Greek sheep's milk cheese with a mild buttery and slightly piquant flavor.

1. Preheat oven to 375°F.

2. Season both sides of chicken with ¾ teaspoon salt, ¼ teaspoon pepper and ⅛ teaspoon ground cinnamon. Heat oil in Dutch oven over medium-high heat. Cook chicken in two batches about 5 minutes per side or until browned. Remove to plate. Drain off all but 2 tablespoons fat.

3. Add onions to Dutch oven; cook and stir 5 minutes or until softened, scraping up browned bits from bottom of pan. Add garlic and remaining ¼ teaspoon ground cinnamon; cook and stir 1 minute. Stir in tomatoes with liquid, broth, cinnamon stick, remaining 1 teaspoon salt and ½ teaspoon pepper; mix well. Return chicken to pan, skin side up, pressing down to partially submerge chicken in sauce.

4. Cover and bake 40 minutes. Remove cover; bake 15 minutes or until chicken is cooked through (165°F). Serve with parsley and cheese, if desired.

Lamb Keftedes with Greek Salad

MAKES 6 SERVINGS

Lamb Keftedes

- **3 slices multigrain bread, finely chopped**
- **½ cup milk**
- **1 cup finely diced onion**
- **2 eggs**
- **1 tablespoon chopped fresh oregano**
- **2 cloves garlic, minced**
- **½ teaspoon salt**
- **1 pound ground lamb**

Greek Salad

- **1½ cups diced cucumber**
- **1½ cups diced tomatoes**
- **Juice of 1 lemon**
- **2 teaspoons olive oil**
- **¼ teaspoon salt**
- **⅛ teaspoon black pepper**

1. Line baking sheet with parchment paper. Combine bread and milk in large bowl; toss to coat. Let stand until liquid is absorbed and bread is fully soaked.

2. Stir in onion, eggs, oregano, garlic and ½ teaspoon salt. Add lamb; mix well. Shape mixture into 36 (½-inch) balls. Place on prepared baking sheet. Refrigerate 30 minutes.

3. Meanwhile, combine cucumber, tomatoes, lemon juice, oil, ¼ teaspoon salt and pepper in medium bowl; set aside.

4. Preheat oven to 400°F. Bake meatballs 20 minutes or until cooked through (160°F), turning halfway through. Serve with salad.

Lemon Rosemary Chicken and Potatoes

MAKES 4 SERVINGS

4 bone-in chicken breasts

½ cup lemon juice

6 tablespoons olive oil, divided

6 cloves garlic, minced, divided

2 tablespoons plus 1 teaspoon chopped fresh rosemary leaves *or* 2¼ teaspoons dried rosemary, divided

1½ teaspoons salt, divided

2 pounds unpeeled small red potatoes, cut into quarters

1 large onion, cut into 2-inch chunks

¼ teaspoon black pepper

1. Place chicken in large resealable food storage bag. Combine lemon juice, 3 tablespoons oil, 3 cloves garlic, 1 tablespoon rosemary and ½ teaspoon salt in small bowl; pour over chicken. Seal bag; turn to coat. Refrigerate several hours or overnight.

2. Preheat oven to 400°F. Combine potatoes and onion in roasting pan. Combine remaining 3 tablespoons oil, 3 cloves garlic, 1 tablespoon rosemary, 1 teaspoon salt and pepper in small bowl; mix well. Pour over vegetables; toss to coat.

3. Drain chicken; discard marinade. Arrange chicken in pan with vegetables in single layer; sprinkle with remaining 1 teaspoon rosemary.

4. Roast about 50 minutes or until potatoes are tender and chicken is cooked through (165°F). Season with additional salt and pepper.

Lemon-Garlic Salmon with Tzatziki Sauce

MAKES 4 SERVINGS

1 cup plain Greek yogurt

½ cup diced cucumber

2 tablespoons fresh lemon juice, divided

1 teaspoon grated lemon peel, divided

1 teaspoon minced garlic, divided

¾ teaspoon salt, divided

¼ teaspoon black pepper

4 skinless salmon fillets (4 ounces each)

1. Combine yogurt, cucumber, 1 tablespoon lemon juice, ½ teaspoon lemon peel, ½ teaspoon garlic and ½ teaspoon salt in medium bowl until combined. Cover and refrigerate until ready to serve.

2. Combine remaining 1 tablespoon lemon juice, ½ teaspoon lemon peel, ½ teaspoon garlic, remaining ¼ teaspoon salt and pepper in small bowl; mix well. Rub evenly onto salmon.

3. Heat nonstick grill pan over medium-high heat. Cook salmon 5 minutes per side or until fish begins to flake when tested with fork. Serve with tzatziki sauce.

Sheet Pan Mediterranean Chicken

MAKES 6 SERVINGS

¼ cup olive oil

4 cloves garlic, thinly sliced

1 tablespoon red wine vinegar

2 teaspoons salt

1½ teaspoons smoked paprika

1 teaspoon dried oregano

½ teaspoon black pepper

6 boneless skinless chicken thighs (about 2 pounds)

2 cans (about 15 ounces each) chickpeas, rinsed and drained

3 pints grape tomatoes

½ cup pitted Kalamata olives, cut into halves

¾ cup (3 ounces) crumbled feta cheese

½ cup chopped fresh parsley

Hot cooked orzo

1. Preheat oven to 425°F. Line baking sheet with foil or spray with nonstick cooking spray.

2. Whisk oil, garlic, vinegar, salt, smoked paprika, oregano and pepper in large bowl until well blended. Add chicken, chickpeas, tomatoes and olives; stir to coat. Spread mixture on prepared baking sheet. (Baking sheet will be very full.)

3. Bake 18 to 20 minutes or until chicken is cooked through (165°F) and tomatoes are beginning to burst. *Turn oven to broil;* broil 2 to 3 minutes or until chicken begins to brown.

4. Sprinkle with cheese and parsley. Serve with orzo.

Lemon-Garlic Shish Kabobs

MAKES 6 SERVINGS

1½ pounds boneless lamb leg, trimmed and cut into 1-inch pieces

¼ cup olive oil

2 tablespoons lemon juice

4 cloves garlic, minced

2 tablespoons chopped fresh oregano *or* 2 teaspoons dried oregano

½ teaspoon salt

½ teaspoon black pepper

1 red or yellow bell pepper, cut into 1-inch pieces

1 small zucchini, cut into 1-inch pieces

1 yellow squash, cut into 1-inch pieces

1 small red onion, cut into ½-inch wedges

8 ounces white or cremini mushrooms, stems trimmed

1. Place lamb in large resealable food storage bag. Combine oil, lemon juice, garlic, oregano, salt and black pepper in small bowl; pour over lamb. Seal bag; turn to coat. Marinate in refrigerator 1 to 4 hours, turning once.

2. Prepare grill for direct cooking over medium-high heat.

3. Drain lamb, reserving marinade. Alternately thread lamb, bell pepper, zucchini, yellow squash, onion and mushrooms onto 12 (10-inch) skewers.* Brush all sides with reserved marinade; discard remaining marinade.

4. Grill kabobs, covered, 10 to 13 minutes or to desired doneness, turning occasionally.

If using wooden skewers, soak in water 30 minutes to prevent burning.

Chicken Cacciatore

MAKES 4 TO 6 SERVINGS

1 tablespoon olive oil

1 whole chicken (3 to 3½ pounds), cut into 8 pieces

4 ounces mushrooms, finely chopped

1 medium onion, chopped

1 clove garlic, minced

½ cup dry white wine

1 tablespoon plus 1½ teaspoons white wine vinegar

1 can (about 14 ounces) crushed tomatoes

½ cup chicken broth

1 teaspoon dried basil

½ teaspoon dried marjoram

½ teaspoon salt

⅛ teaspoon black pepper

8 Italian- or Greek-style pitted black olives, halved

1 tablespoon chopped fresh parsley

Hot cooked pasta

1. Heat oil in large skillet over medium-high heat. Cook chicken in batches 8 minutes per side or until browned. Transfer browned chicken to Dutch oven with tongs.

2. Add mushrooms and onion to drippings in skillet; cook and stir over medium heat 5 minutes or until onion is soft. Add garlic; cook and stir 30 seconds. Add wine and vinegar; cook over medium-high heat 5 minutes or until liquid is almost evaporated. Stir in tomatoes, broth, basil, marjoram, salt and pepper. Bring to a boil; boil 2 minutes.

3. Pour sauce over chicken in Dutch oven. Bring to a boil over medium-high heat; reduce heat to low. Cover and simmer 25 minutes or until chicken is tender and juices run clear when pierced with fork. Remove chicken with slotted spatula to serving dish; keep warm.

4. Bring sauce to a boil over medium-high heat; boil, uncovered, 5 minutes. Add olives and parsley; cook 1 minute. Serve chicken and sauce over pasta.

Sides & Vegetables

Italian-Style Roasted Vegetables

MAKES 6 SERVINGS

1 eggplant, cut into chunks

1 zucchini, cut into chunks

1 red bell pepper, cut into chunks

1 yellow bell pepper, cut into chunks

1 onion, cut into chunks

2 tablespoons olive oil

1 teaspoon balsamic vinegar

1 teaspoon minced garlic

½ teaspoon salt

½ teaspoon dried basil

½ teaspoon dried oregano

¼ teaspoon red pepper flakes

1. Preheat oven to 425°F.

2. Combine vegetables in large bowl. Drizzle with oil and vinegar; sprinkle with garlic, salt, basil, oregano and red pepper; toss until well blended. Spread on two large baking sheets.

3. Roast 25 to 30 minutes or until vegetables are tender and browned, stirring once.

Greek Rice

MAKES 6 SERVINGS

2 tablespoons butter

1¾ cups uncooked long grain rice

2 cans (about 14 ounces each) vegetable broth

1 teaspoon Greek seasoning

1 teaspoon dried oregano

½ teaspoon salt

1 cup pitted kalamata olives, drained and chopped

¾ cup chopped roasted red peppers

Crumbled feta cheese (optional)

Chopped fresh parsley (optional)

1. Melt butter in large nonstick skillet over medium heat. Add rice; cook and stir 4 minutes or until golden brown. Add broth, Greek seasoning, oregano and salt; bring to a boil. Reduce heat to low; cover and simmer about 15 minutes or until broth is absorbed and rice is tender. Remove from heat; let stand, covered, 5 minutes.

2. Stir in olives and roasted red peppers. Top with cheese and parsley, if desired.

White Beans and Tomatoes

MAKES 4 TO 6 SERVINGS

1 tablespoon olive oil

1 medium onion, chopped

1 tablespoon tomato paste

2 teaspoons minced garlic

2 teaspoons dried oregano

1 teaspoon salt

½ teaspoon black pepper (optional)

2 cans (about 15 ounces each) cannellini beans, rinsed and drained

1 can (about 14 ounces) crushed tomatoes

½ cup water

1. Heat oil in medium saucepan over medium-high heat. Add onion; cook and stir 5 minutes or until softened. Add tomato paste, garlic, oregano, salt and black pepper, if desired; cook and stir 1 minute. Add beans, tomatoes and water; mix well.

2. Reduce heat to medium-low. Partially cover and cook about 20 minutes or until beans are saucy and heated through.

Greek White Bean Risotto

MAKES 4 TO 6 SERVINGS

6 cups vegetable broth

¼ cup olive oil

1 onion, chopped

3 cloves garlic, minced

1½ cups uncooked arborio rice

2 teaspoons dried oregano

1 teaspoon salt

⅓ cup dry white wine

⅓ cup finely chopped sun-dried tomatoes

1 cup canned cannellini beans, rinsed and drained

¾ cup (3 ounces) crumbled feta cheese

⅓ cup grated Parmesan cheese

1 teaspoon lemon juice

½ teaspoon black pepper

1. Bring broth to a boil in large saucepan. Reduce heat to low to maintain a simmer.

2. Heat oil in large saucepan over medium heat. Add onion; cook and stir 5 minutes or until softened. Add garlic; cook and stir 1 minute. Add rice, oregano and salt; cook and stir 2 to 3 minutes or until rice is translucent. Add wine; cook and stir 2 to 3 minutes or until absorbed. Stir in sun-dried tomatoes.

3. Add broth, ½ cup at a time, stirring frequently until broth is absorbed before adding next ½ cup. Continue adding broth and stirring until rice is tender and mixture is creamy, about 20 to 25 minutes total.

4. Stir beans into risotto; cook 1 minute, stirring constantly. Remove from heat. Stir in cheeses, lemon juice and pepper. Cover; let stand 5 minutes. Stir before serving.

Roasted Rainbow Carrots with Sweet Tahini

MAKES 4 SERVINGS

Carrots

- 2 pounds rainbow carrots, peeled and halved lengthwise if large
- 2 tablespoons olive oil
- 1½ teaspoons salt
- 1 teaspoon ground cumin
- ½ teaspoon dried thyme
- ½ teaspoon Aleppo pepper or black pepper

Sauce

- 2 tablespoons tahini
- 1 tablespoon lemon juice
- 1 tablespoon maple syrup or honey
- ¼ teaspoon salt
- Dash ground cumin
- 2 tablespoons water

1. Preheat oven to 400°F. Place carrots on baking sheet; drizzle with oil. Combine 1½ teaspoons salt, 1 teaspoon ground cumin, thyme and pepper in small bowl. Sprinkle over carrots; toss to coat carrots with oil and seasonings.

2. Roast 20 minutes or until carrots are fork-tender and charred, turning once. Place on serving plate.

3. Meanwhile for sauce, whisk tahini, lemon juice, maple syrup, ¼ teaspoon salt and dash cumin in small bowl. Whisk in water until smooth. Drizzle over carrots.

Chicken and Vegetable Risotto

MAKES 4 SERVINGS

6 cups chicken broth

2 cups sliced mushrooms

1 onion, chopped

¼ cup olive oil

4 cloves garlic, minced

1½ cups uncooked arborio rice

1 teaspoon salt

¼ cup dry white wine

1 cup chopped cooked chicken

2 cups cooked broccoli florets

4 plum tomatoes, seeded and chopped

¼ cup finely chopped fresh parsley

¼ cup finely chopped fresh basil

½ teaspoon black pepper

¼ cup grated Parmesan or Romano cheese

1. Bring broth to a boil in medium saucepan. Reduce heat to low to maintain a simmer.

2. Heat large saucepan over medium heat. Add mushrooms; cook and stir 5 minutes or until tender. Add onion, oil and garlic; cook and stir 5 minutes or until onion is tender. Add rice and salt; cook and stir 2 to 3 minutes or until rice is translucent. Add wine; cook and stir 1 to 2 minutes or until absorbed.

3. Add broth, ½ cup at a time, stirring frequently until broth is absorbed before adding next ½ cup. Continue adding broth and stirring until rice is tender and mixture is creamy, about 20 to 25 minutes total.

4. Add chicken, broccoli, tomatoes, parsley, basil and pepper; cook and stir 2 to 3 minutes or until heated through. Sprinkle with cheese.

Mediterranean Vegetable Bake

MAKES 4 SERVINGS

2 tomatoes, sliced

1 small red onion, sliced

1 medium zucchini, sliced

1 small eggplant, sliced

1 small yellow squash, sliced

1 large portobello mushroom, sliced

2 cloves garlic, finely chopped

3 tablespoons olive oil

2 teaspoons chopped fresh rosemary leaves

⅔ cup dry white wine

Salt and black pepper

1. Preheat oven to 350°F. Grease bottom of oval casserole or 13×9-inch baking dish.

2. Arrange slices of vegetables in rows, alternating different types and overlapping slices in baking dish to make attractive arrangement; sprinkle evenly with garlic. Combine oil and rosemary in small bowl; drizzle over vegetables.

3. Pour wine over vegetables; season with salt and pepper. Cover loosely with foil. Bake 20 minutes. Uncover; bake 10 to 15 minutes or until vegetables are tender.

Grilled Vegetables with Polenta

MAKES 4 SERVINGS

2 large bell peppers, quartered

2 medium zucchini, cut horizontally into ½-inch-thick pieces

1 pound asparagus (about 20 spears)

1 large red onion, cut into ½-inch-thick rounds

¼ cup olive oil

2 teaspoons salt, divided

1 teaspoon Italian seasoning

1 teaspoon black pepper, divided

4 cups water

1 cup uncooked polenta

4 ounces crumbled goat cheese

1. Arrange bell peppers, zucchini and asparagus in single layer on one or two baking sheets. To hold onion together securely, pierce slices horizontally with metal skewers. Add to baking sheet. Combine oil, 1 teaspoon salt, Italian seasoning and ½ teaspoon black pepper in small bowl. Brush mixture generously over vegetables, turning to coat all sides.

2. Prepare grill for direct cooking. Meanwhile, bring water to a boil with remaining 1 teaspoon salt in large saucepan. Gradually whisk in polenta. Reduce heat to medium. Cook, stirring constantly, until polenta thickens and begins to pull away from side of pan. Stir in remaining ½ teaspoon black pepper. Keep warm.

3. Grill vegetables over medium-high heat, covered, 10 to 15 minutes or until tender, turning once. Place bell peppers in large bowl. Cover; let stand 5 minutes to loosen skin. When cool enough to handle, peel off charred skin. Cut all vegetables into bite-size pieces.

4. Serve polenta topped with vegetables and sprinkled with goat cheese.

Mushroom and Romano Risotto

MAKES 4 SERVINGS

6 cups vegetable broth	1 teaspoon salt
8 ounces sliced mushrooms	½ cup Madeira wine
½ cup chopped shallots	½ cup grated Romano cheese
½ cup chopped onion	3 tablespoons butter, softened
3 tablespoons olive oil	3 tablespoons chopped fresh parsley
3 cloves garlic, minced	¼ teaspoon black pepper
1½ cups uncooked arborio rice	

1. Bring broth to a boil in medium saucepan. Reduce heat to low to maintain a simmer.

2. Heat Dutch oven over medium-high heat. Add mushrooms; cook and stir 6 to 7 minutes or until beginning to brown. Stir in shallots, onion, oil and garlic; cook and stir 2 to 3 minutes or until vegetables begin to soften. Add rice and salt; cook and stir 2 to 3 minutes or until rice is translucent. Add wine; cook and stir 1 to 2 minutes or until absorbed.

3. Add broth, ½ cup at a time, stirring frequently until broth is absorbed before adding next ½ cup. Continue adding broth and stirring until rice is tender and mixture is creamy, about 20 to 25 minutes total.

4. Remove from heat; stir in cheese, butter, parsley and pepper. Serve immediately.

Risi Bisi

MAKES 6 SERVINGS

1 tablespoon olive oil

1 tablespoon butter

¾ cup chopped onion

2 cloves garlic, minced

1½ cups long grain rice

1 teaspoon salt

¾ teaspoon Italian seasoning

3½ cups water

½ cup thawed frozen peas

¼ cup grated Parmesan cheese

¼ cup toasted pine nuts (optional)

1. Heat oil and butter in medium saucepan over medium-high heat. Add onion and garlic; cook and stir 5 minutes or until softened. Add rice, salt and seasoning; cook and stir 1 minute. Add water; bring to a boil. Reduce heat to low. Cover and simmer 12 to 15 minutes or until water is absorbed and rice is tender.

2. Sir in peas and cheese; top with pine nuts, if desired.

Mediterranean Red Potatoes

MAKES 4 SERVINGS

4 medium red potatoes, cut into 1-inch pieces

1 small yellow onion, thinly sliced

2 tablespoons olive oil

1 clove garlic, minced

¾ teaspoon Italian seasoning

½ teaspoon salt

¼ teaspoon black pepper

1 tomato, seeded and chopped

½ cup crumbled feta cheese

2 tablespoons chopped black olives

1. Preheat oven to 400°F. Spray baking sheet with nonstick cooking spray.

2. Combine potatoes, onion, oil, garlic, Italian seasoning, salt and pepper in large bowl; toss until well blended. Spread on prepared baking sheet.

3. Bake 25 to 30 minutes or until potatoes are tender and lightly browned. Transfer to serving dish; stir in tomato, cheese and olives.

Couscous and Vegetable Salad

MAKES 4 SERVINGS

4 tablespoons olive oil, divided

1 cup sliced mushrooms

1 yellow or orange bell pepper, chopped

1 onion, chopped

1 stalk celery, chopped

1 clove garlic, minced

1 teaspoon salt

¼ teaspoon dried thyme

¼ teaspoon black pepper

1 cup uncooked pearl couscous

2 cups vegetable broth

8 ounces asparagus, cut into 1-inch pieces

1 cup chopped cooked chicken (optional)

¼ cup quartered grape tomatoes (optional)

1 tablespoon white wine vinegar

1 teaspoon Dijon mustard

2 teaspoons chopped fresh chives

Salt and black pepper

1. Heat 2 tablespoons oil in large skillet over medium-high heat. Add mushrooms, bell pepper, onion, celery, garlic, salt, thyme and black pepper. Cook and stir 6 to 8 minutes or until vegetables are crisp-tender. Stir in couscous; cook and stir 1 minute.

2. Stir in broth; reduce heat to medium-low. Cook about 15 minutes or until couscous is tender, adding asparagus during the last 5 minutes of cooking (stir in water by tablespoons if broth is absorbed and mixture is dry). Transfer to large bowl; stir in chicken and tomatoes, if desired.

3. Whisk remaining 2 tablespoons oil, vinegar, mustard and chives in small bowl until well blended. Season with salt and pepper. Pour over couscous mixture; mix well. Serve warm or chilled.

Index

Index

Index

Index

Metric Conversion Chart

VOLUME MEASUREMENTS (dry)

1/8 teaspoon = 0.5 mL
1/4 teaspoon = 1 mL
1/2 teaspoon = 2 mL
3/4 teaspoon = 4 mL
1 teaspoon = 5 mL
1 tablespoon = 15 mL
2 tablespoons = 30 mL
1/4 cup = 60 mL
1/3 cup = 75 mL
1/2 cup = 125 mL
2/3 cup = 150 mL
3/4 cup = 175 mL
1 cup = 250 mL
2 cups = 1 pint = 500 mL
3 cups = 750 mL
4 cups = 1 quart = 1 L

VOLUME MEASUREMENTS (fluid)

1 fluid ounce (2 tablespoons) = 30 mL
4 fluid ounces (1/2 cup) = 125 mL
8 fluid ounces (1 cup) = 250 mL
12 fluid ounces (1 1/2 cups) = 375 mL
16 fluid ounces (2 cups) = 500 mL

WEIGHTS (mass)

1/2 ounce = 15 g
1 ounce = 30 g
3 ounces = 90 g
4 ounces = 120 g
8 ounces = 225 g
10 ounces = 285 g
12 ounces = 360 g
16 ounces = 1 pound = 450 g

DIMENSIONS

1/16 inch = 2 mm
1/8 inch = 3 mm
1/4 inch = 6 mm
1/2 inch = 1.5 cm
3/4 inch = 2 cm
1 inch = 2.5 cm

OVEN TEMPERATURES

250°F = 120°C
275°F = 140°C
300°F = 150°C
325°F = 160°C
350°F = 180°C
375°F = 190°C
400°F = 200°C
425°F = 220°C
450°F = 230°C

BAKING PAN SIZES

Utensil	Size in Inches/Quarts	Metric Volume	Size in Centimeters
Baking or Cake Pan (square or rectangular)	8×8×2	2 L	20×20×5
	9×9×2	2.5 L	23×23×5
	12×8×2	3 L	30×20×5
	13×9×2	3.5 L	33×23×5
Loaf Pan	8×4×3	1.5 L	20×10×7
	9×5×3	2 L	23×13×7
Round Layer Cake Pan	8×1½	1.2 L	20×4
	9×1½	1.5 L	23×4
Pie Plate	8×1¼	750 mL	20×3
	9×1¼	1 L	23×3
Baking Dish or Casserole	1 quart	1 L	—
	1½ quart	1.5 L	—
	2 quart	2 L	—